WRITING ACROSS THE CURRICULUM IN MIDDLE AND HIGH SCHOOLS

WRITING ACROSS THE CURRICULUM IN MIDDLE AND HIGH SCHOOLS

Rhoda J. Maxwell

University of Wisconsin-Eau Claire

Allyn and Bacon

Boston • London • Toronto • Sydney • Tokyo • Singapore

Copyright © 1996 by Allyn & Bacon
A Simon & Schuster Company
Needham Heights, Massachusetts 02194

Credits:

Series Editor: Virginia Lanigan
Editorial Assistant: Nihad Farooq
Manufacturing Buyer: Aloka Rathnam

Library of Congress Cataloging-in-Publication Data

Maxwell, Rhoda J.
    Writing across the curriculum in middle and high schools / Rhoda
J. Maxwell.
        p.   cm.
    Includes bibliographical references and index.
    ISBN 0-205-15325-9
    1. English language—Composition and exercises—Study and teaching
(Secondary)   2. Interdisciplinary approach in education.   I. Title.
LB1631.M3936   1996
428'.0071'2—dc20   95-456
                                                                              CIP

Printed in the United States of America
10   9   8   7   6   5   4   3   2   1   99   98   97   96   95

To Clinton, Ginny, and Sara
With love and gratitude

CONTENTS

PREFACE

Writing Across the Curriculum in Middle and High Schools is designed as a text for education majors and minors in all subjects, as well as a resource for experienced teachers. The initial idea for this book came from the writing project I directed for several years. In that project, we explored ways to incorporate writing across the curriculum. Gradually, that focus shifted to using writing as a means of learning across the curriculum. Writing to learn is the central theme of this book.

Writing helps students learn in many ways: recalling, revising, organizing, connecting ideas, and discovering new information. Writing assists learning from the time a teacher first introduces a concept until the final evaluation of a unit. The writing activities presented here can be used throughout a teaching unit to recognize prior knowledge, motivate, increase understanding, organize new information, and make meaningful connections. Through writing, students construct knowledge and become active learners.

The writing levels and the writing process provide the structure for the activities. This is not a collection of random ideas to include writing across the curriculum but, rather, a way of helping students become involved in their learning. The more students are involved in a task, the easier they learn and the longer they retain what they learn.

The development and use of writing levels has been part of my research and teaching since the late 1970s. I used the writing process in my first years of teaching science, English, and social studies in middle school and soon became overwhelmed with the load of papers I dragged home every evening. I did not want to give up any of the writing activities; in fact, I kept adding more. Something had to change. The suggestions I heard or read seemed out of touch with my classroom and lacked a systematic approach to evaluation. Basing my original work on speech theory, I devised the levels-of-writing approach for all of the writing assignments. The writing levels solve the problem of evaluation, a serious problem for content-area teachers who want to include writing to learn in their classrooms.

One chapter is devoted to describing the levels of writing, which are then incorporated throughout the book.

Research and theory provide the backbone of this book, while the general focus is practical application. The writing activities come from my own classrooms and from other teachers across the country. Student examples from middle and high schools illustrate the writing process, the writing levels, and various types of writing. Three chapters highlight writing for specific curricular areas, and the rest cover cross-curriculum areas.

The questions at the beginning of each chapter are designed to elicit discussion about students' own experiences and provide a context for the material that follows. The questions and suggested activities at the end of each chapter help students connect the chapter content with their future teaching experiences.

Suggestions for teaching include small groups, whole class, and individual work. Students learn from each other as well as from the teacher, and the design of the activities promotes interactive learning. The last chapter covers interdisciplinary units for a variety of situations: individual classrooms, team teaching, and cooperative planning.

I am grateful to all the teachers and students who have shared their work and ideas and to the many writing project teachers who have supported me throughout this project. A special thanks goes to my education students for their enthusiasm and talent. Also, my thanks to Rebecca Olien for her careful and insightful reading; to my graduate assistants, Mary Haroldson and Jessica Wilson, for their invaluable help; and to Virginia Lanigan and Nihad Farooq at Allyn and Bacon for their encouragement and kindness.

I want, too, to thank the reviewers for their helpful suggestions: Joan Shiring, John Zelazek, Eugene Kim, Michael Angelotti, Betty McEady-Gillead, Susan R. McIntyre, and Margot C. Papworth.

R.J.M.

WRITING ACROSS THE CURRICULUM IN MIDDLE AND HIGH SCHOOLS

1

WRITING ACROSS THE CURRICULUM

Schools exist primarily to teach people basic literacy skills which are prerequisites for learning basic thinking skills, which are in turn prerequisites for civilized existence as we know it. If we want schools to do more than teach the basics of thinking—if, in addition, we want schools to teach critical, independent thinking—then we must question the ill-defined role of writing throughout the curriculum.—TOBY FULWILER, 1987

Prereading Questions

1. What writing did you do in the elementary grades?
2. How did writing change in amount or kind from junior to senior high?
3. How is writing in school related to writing outside of school?
4. What is your favorite kind of writing?
5. In what ways might writing help a person to learn?

Introduction

Writing, once thought of as belonging solely to the English class, is now used throughout the curriculum from elementary grades to college classes. The reason for the change is that we realize writing helps students learn the content of every subject. We include writing across the curriculum not to add more work to an already crowded curriculum but to improve the learning of content. Writing is not used in content areas so that students will improve their writing skills, but because students understand content better when writing becomes part of their learning activities. In *How Writing Shapes Thinking*, Langer and Applebee (1978) explain that any type of written response improves learning and retention rather than reading and listening without writing (p. 130).

Writing has been used in subjects other than English for many years, but largely for reports and informational writing. Langer and Applebee explain that the teaching of writing has "been prescriptive and product centered" (p. 6). Most writing was done to show the teacher how much the student had learned. On occasion this is appropriate, but when we compare the uses of writing in general to the way writing is used in school, we see that we are not fully utilizing the benefits of writing. Writing enhances learning in all areas because it helps students synthesize knowledge.

Writing in Every Subject

Writing across the curriculum "has come to mean drawing upon writing as a resource for skill building and for learning" (Winchell & Elder, 1994, p. 273). When including writing in content subjects, it is vital to remember that we must keep content at the center of the writing process (Tchudi & Yates, 1983, p. 8). For teachers who want to incorporate writing, the central question is: What do we want students to learn? The issue is not what writing to teach. Writing in every subject helps students learn the subject's content. Many elements of writing are similar regardless of whether the class is art, history, music, or physical education. In every class, using examples to illustrate a point is important. The same is true for using details, organizing material for clarity, backing up statements with evidence, using specific language, and writing coherently.

Some differences do exist from one subject to another. A subject may have its own specialized vocabulary. Audiences vary, as do the purposes of assignments. The form of various types of writing changes from subject to subject. In general, however, the similarities outweigh the differences.

More writing is involved in English than in other subjects because writing is inherently part of the content. A wider variety of writing activities is used in English. Other content teachers might have students write drama, fiction, and poetry, but that would be the exception. All teachers, however, find journal writing appropriate. Traditionally, teachers of subjects other than English, if they used writing at all, had students only write reports. The argument is made throughout this book that writing belongs in every subject, in a variety of forms and for a variety of purposes.

Purposes of Writing

The writing we do in our everyday life fulfills many purposes. We write to communicate when we send letters, leave messages, or write explanations. We use writing as a memory aid when we write lists of things to do, groceries to buy, or errands to run. We jot down a name of someone we meet, the time to meet some-one, the name of a song, a friend's birthday. We use writing for organization when we reorder our list of things to do from most important to least, or when we group our errands to save time and gas. We use writing to help us make sense of new knowledge when we take notes. The purposes writing fulfills in our personal life are related to the reasons writing is appropriate across the curriculum.

As in real life, we use writing in school to communicate, memorize, and or-ganize. Students can write letters to an outside audience—for instance, busi-nesses, newspapers, other classes, or parents. They might write letters to thank someone or to invite a speaker to the class. Summaries of readings communicate information to the teacher and their peers; homework assignments communicate understandings; journals provide a place for informal communication. To help with memory in school, students write lists, assignments, and notes from a lec-ture. The act of writing is a memory aid because it entails a higher degree of in-volvement than listening or reading. Having our thoughts visible through writ-ing, so we can see where we need to rearrange, combine, or expand, helps us to understand and accomplish organization. We write to discover what we know and what we need to learn. "Writing's greatest gift is the ability to help us learn" (Moore, 1994, p. 290).

Studies show that writing increases recall and understanding of information. When students organize their ideas through writing, the information makes more sense to them. A math teacher describes the results of using writing in her class as helping students practice writing in a meaningful way so that they understood their problem-solving process well enough to communicate their ideas on paper (Fortescue, 1994, p. 577).

Because of the importance of writing in learning, one might expect a high per-centage of class time to be devoted to writing activities, but this is not the case. Arthur Applebee found in observational studies that the amount of time teachers spent on prewriting averaged just over three minutes (1981, p. 74). Writing itself was more a "task of mechanically slotting in the missing information" than of stu-dents producing meaningful text (p. 99). Not only is the amount of time spent on writing minimal, but the type of writing is prescriptive and restrictive. Conse-quently, it is not too surprising to read reports that relatively few eleventh-grade students could write adequate responses to analytical writing tasks. Even fewer could write an argument to back up a point of view (Applebee, Langer, & Mullis, 1986, p. 10).

The amount of writing in subject areas other than English increases between grades 4 and 8 and then decreases again in high school (Applebee et al., 1986, p. 10). Yet high school is the time when writing in content areas should increase to help students prepare for future jobs. Writing is commonly required in the work force to prepare reports, evaluations, directions, technical reports, and busi-ness letters. People have to know how to communicate to achieve success in the workplace. Tchudi and Yates (1983) contend that writing about content has a practical payoff: "it gives practice for real-world writing" (p. 7). Writing is used for (1) gaining knowledge, (2) reviewing and consolidating what is learned, and (3) reformulating and extending ideas and experiences (Langer & Applebee, 1978, p. 136).

Writing as Thinking

Critical thinking is a broad term that can be defined in a variety of ways. Stephen Wilhoit describes it as "including knowledge of subject matter, ability to analyze and evaluate ideas, and willingness to apply these skills when forming and defending assertions" (1993, p. 125). Writing is one of three main ways of enhancing the thinking of students; the others are questioning techniques and information processing (Marzano, 1993, p. 154). The writing process teaches skills through "modeling, coaching, practice, and response," which provide opportunities for students to become independent reflective thinkers (p. 129). Karen Ernst supports the connection between writing and thinking: "Writing leads our students to the process of discovery, learning, and thinking" (1994, p. 51).

We want our students to develop the abilities to evaluate sources, information, and points of view in order to make careful, well-thought-out decisions. Writing helps with this because when we put thoughts and feelings on paper, we have a product to reflect on. The writing process is "inherently an act of generating ideas that we can then reflect on" (Stout, 1993, p. 37). With writing, we can clarify information, see relationships, and make connections. "[W]riting assists learning because it provides a visual product that permits opportunities for revising" (Davis, Rooze, & Runnels, 1992, p. 393)—revising thoughts, opinions, and feelings.

Sharing writing in response groups helps students come to understand other points of view as well as reflect on their own. To be a critical thinker means to question what one hears, reads, or believes. "Students need to learn to suspend disbelief or belief long enough to make sure they understand incoming information before judging it" (Bacon & Thayer-Bacon, 1993, p. 182). To become critical decision makers is a lifelong goal that will serve students well.

"Knowing how to think, to apply, analyze, synthesize and evaluate are primary skills" (Doney, Lephardt, & Trebby, 1993, p. 297). If students can move from acquiring knowledge to knowing how to learn and apply what they know to a variety of contexts, they have developed higher order thinking skills. No longer is "a brainful of facts" enough; we must learn to think critically (Chiras, 1992, p. 468).

Langer and Applebee state that "Thinking skills are best taught when related to some content" (1978, p. 4). "Many years of research suggest that better learning occurs when students *use* writing to think about what they are learning in various classes" (Applebee et al., 1986, p. 12). Critical thinking has to be connected with learning about something, not taught in abstract terms; just as writing has to be writing for a specific reason. Writing helps develop critical thinking, and both are learned through content material.

Types of Writing

Most of the writing done in schools is expository and argumentative. Little attention is paid to the nature of the writing task or the demands the task makes on writers. Young people in school are not professional writers, and the sophistication of exposition and argumentation is well beyond their developmental level. To improve the writing ability of students, the types of writing must change to fit more closely students' characteristics and the purposes of writing in real-world situations.

Researchers since the mid-1960s have looked for more appropriate types of writing for students and for ways to help students improve their ability to write. James Britton and his colleagues from the University of London Institute of Education developed a descriptive classification that helps us understand types of writing and stages of growth and development in students. When they began looking at the kinds of writing students did in London schools, they needed a more satisfying way of classifying pieces of writing than the traditional ones of narrative, description, exposition, and argumentation (Britton, Burgess, Martin, McLeod, & Rosen, 1975, p. 1). The problem with this system, originally designed in 1776, is that the writing is "profoundly prescriptive" and has little to do with the writing process (p. 4).

The group looked at the development of the ability to write as the basis for a new classification. They drew on Edward Sapir's theory of speech and, in particular, the expressive nature of speech. When the need to communicate to a wider audience comes up, speech becomes more explicit and formal (p. 11). This "shifting-focus" model of writing comes, too, from Dell Hymes's work. Hymes developed a "functional classification" that explains language functions in terms of "actual human lives" (1972, p. 43). People develop a specialization in language based on specific situations and functional varieties. In other words, the degree of formality and speech patterns people use depends on social context and on the abilities of the speaker.

Britton and his colleagues looked at the development of writing in its relation to the development of thinking. They took into account the psychological processes and social setting that determine the functions of written language (Britton et al., 1975, p. 6). Their model represents three function categories of writing based on distinction between language as a *means* (used to inform, instruct, persuade) and language as an *end* (used for no specific reason). The categories are represented in a diagram, as follows (p. 81):

TRANSACTIONAL—EXPRESSIVE—POETIC
(as a means) ——————————— (as an end)

Expressive is the first type of writing a child does. It correlates with expressive speech, where children make sense of their experiences by talking about them. A child's first attempts at figuring things out are expressed as *inner speech,* a term Lev Vygotsky used to describe the flow of thought into language as verbal thought becomes internalized, like thinking out loud (1962, p. 15). The audience is often the child alone but may include trusted adults. In sharing experiences with others, we make those experiences real to ourselves (Britton, 1975, p. 6). We see this in young children when they talk about what happened or why something happened. We also use expressive language as adults when we are trying to understand an event or feeling; like young children, we, too, talk experiences over with an audience we know well. Expressive writing is a way of figuring things out, of trying to make sense of information, and allows transactional writing to succeed.

Transactional writing, often called getting-down-to-business writing, is for a wider audience. Its function is to provide information. We transact with others by explaining, summarizing, presenting new information, showing what we know. Because of the wider audience, the writing is more formal and relies on writing conventions to help the readers understand the meaning. Transactional writing should "address an audience beyond the writer"—for example, a business memo or scholarly paper (Murdick & Grinstead, 1992, p. 59).

Poetic writing uses language as an art medium. The words are selected to make an arrangement, a formal pattern. It "exists for its own sake and not as a means of achieving something else" (Britton et al., 1975, 90).

James Moffett describes the distinction between expressive and transactional writing as the increasing distance between speaker and listener. The more abstract the writing, the greater distance between writer and reader. Moffett compares the amount of distance as a scale of I/you in the sense of audience. The *I* is writing for oneself, and the *you* is writing to someone else. Compared to Britton's diagram, the same idea is expressed as the difference between expressive (the *I*) and transactional (the *you*) (1975, pp. 32–33). Expressive writing includes thoughts, feelings and moods; transactional writing includes recording and sharing information, note-taking, summaries, and essays (Freedman, 1993, p. 6).

The concept of classification presented in this model can help teachers expand their use of writing in schools, rather than writing only to fulfill mechanistic, trivial purposes that do not generate ideas, such as recall, fill-in-the-blanks, and true/false questions (Moore, 1994, p. 289). Most school writing is transactional, especially at the secondary level; the benefits of expressive writing are often ignored. "Expressive writing does not look much like school writing" (Stout, 1993, p. 38). The result is that young writers write for the teacher or for an unknown, unspecified audience, creating a sense of distance between audience and writer.

The more involved a writer is in the writing task, the more likely the writing is to be lively, interesting, and meaningful. We all do a better job at something we feel involved and interested in. Britton states that the quality of student involvement relates to expressive uses of language (1975, p. 7). Unless students have the opportunity to use expressive writing in secondary schools, involving them in writing tasks is difficult. Using expressive writing also gives students the sense that what they think and know matters to the teacher. A classroom atmosphere that creates dialogue between teacher and student, as well as between students, sets the stage for writing to occur and, consequently, to improve.

Traits of Middle and High School Students

Students of middle school age are different developmentally and socially from high school students. Because this book is written for teachers of middle and high school students, a look at these differences seems appropriate. Although students across grade levels all use a process approach to writing, the differences in their abilities and understanding are great. An eighth-grader and a junior may even receive the same writing assignment, but the end results are not similar. The distinctions go far beyond the developmental stage. Young adolescents in grades 6 through 8 are characterized by impulsiveness, impatience with restrictions, self-consciousness, moodiness, and easy embarrassment (National Association of Secondary School Principals). Young adolescents do not have the attention span of older students, and they work best if teachers provide hands-on experiences. Activities that include movement, if only moving from group work to individual study, help keep them on task.

The self-esteem of both middle and high school students is vulnerable, so teachers must be careful not to show their work unless the students agree beforehand. Evaluation is always private, although students themselves almost always share the information. Middle school students have a well-developed (one could say overdeveloped) sense of fair play, so teachers need to explain their expectations carefully and keep students informed of any changes in plans. Middle school educator John Arnold writes that the most important way to help middle schoolers is to "positively affect the day to day interactions in the classroom" (1985, p. 1). The responsibility rests with teachers.

The payoff is that students in this age group are full of energy, interested in activities, willing to try new things, and love to talk. In *Seeking Diversity* Linda Rief writes, "Working with teenagers is not easy" (1992, p. 90). It takes patience, humor, and love. It is important to support them by "laughing with them, respecting them, and helping them find out what's good about their lives" (p. 91).

Learning Styles

Learning styles affect how we approach problem solving, how we retain information, and how we learn in general. Some people learn best in the morning, others at night. Some learn best by listening, others by reading, others by visual approaches. Students who cannot sit still through a class might have a learning style that requires movement. We can assume we have a variety of learning styles in every class. It is important for a teacher to know her or his own learning style because we tend to teach the way we learn. If we learn by listening, we tend to rely on lecture to get ideas across. This method works well only with students who have learning styles similar to ours.

To assure optimum learning in our classes, teachers must incorporate several approaches into their teaching. For example, when teachers first give an assignment, they need to explain it verbally, write major points on a chalkboard or overhead, and then have students write it in their learning log. Having students write it themselves works better than handing out a description of the assignment. The more students handle the information, the longer they retain it. Then students meet in groups or pairs to compare what they wrote and verify with each other that they understand the teacher's expectations.

When every student begins an assignment with a solid understanding, the teacher's work as well as the students' is greatly simplified. The same approach— teacher talk, writing important points, student writing, and sharing information in groups, with the addition of reading—creates a learning environment that works best for most students. Add the use of nonprint material in presenting information, and we have created a class favorable to a wide variety of learning styles, regardless of our own preference.

Classroom Environment

An optimum environment for learning is based on mutual respect between students and teachers. Although many factors are beyond our control, we want to establish, as much as possible, a bond of trust. Writing, in particular, needs a supportive atmosphere; it takes courage to expose our thoughts and feelings through writing. The social climate must be supportive of written expression. Adolescents are especially vulnerable because of their struggle for self-esteem and their fear or expectation that teachers might criticize them.

Classroom environment is made up of many elements. The most important is the knowledge that students are respected. Student behavior can be frustrating for teachers, but the underlying assumption that guides teacher planning and behavior must reflect respect for students. Evidence of this respect can appear in several ways.

- Listening to students and believing they have important things to say
- Valuing their right to opinions whether we agree or not
- Acknowledging the problems students have outside of school
- Being as polite to students as we are to people outside of class
- Understanding their need to socialize
- Being realistic in behavior expectations

Teachers who listen to students have tremendous impact on the climate of the class. Several studies show that teachers listen very little compared to how much they talk. The more involved students are in what is going on in class, the more they learn. Talking is an important part of that involvement, partly because it eases boredom. Also, by including student talk in the learning process, teachers show that student responses and opinions are valued. "Improved communication between students and teachers is essential for developing critical thinking skills" (Nelson, 1989). We need to focus on providing time for talk and not look for answers to specific questions. Teachers should emphasize *how* and *why* rather than *who, what, where,* and *when* (Nelson, 1989). Students need to speak and write more in order to practice their abilities to think.

An efficient way to plan for student talk is to include group work in class activities. Expecting students to work individually all the time goes against normal social behavior for everyone. Teachers, too, like to talk, and teacher meetings illustrate the importance of sharing conversation. We often set up behavior guidelines for students that teachers themselves would never follow. Teachers can focus group work so that students discuss the intended topic by sharing the highlights or summary of their conversation. Group work facilitates students learning from each other as well as from the teacher; and unless we provide this opportunity, we are missing a powerful resource.

Students' lives outside of school can be difficult. Resources within the school system can help, and teachers need to be alert to the need to refer students to appropriate people. It helps to be aware of the problems students can have with family situations, drugs, alcohol, illness, taxing outside jobs, and the myriad of societal ills that create serious problems for young people. A student who falls asleep in class may have been up all night with a sick family member or may have worked most of the night because of economic necessity.

We want our classrooms to be safe havens from the turmoil of troubled lives, a place where students' thoughts and ideas are respected and listened to, where they are valued as unique individuals. We cannot do much to change the world, but as teachers we do have control over what goes on in our classrooms.

Planning for Writing Across the Curriculum

When including writing in the curriculum, we begin by determining the content objectives and then develop writing ideas that help students learn the concepts of the content area. Writing activities help students organize information from a variety of sources. By writing, students can connect new knowledge to what they already know and make sense of what they are learning.

Richard Prawat explains that we have to replace the telling–listening relationship that exists between many teachers and students with a dynamic model of interaction (1992, p. 357). It is important for teachers to honor the efforts students make to learn and create a classroom where students are free to make mistakes (p. 380). This desired change in focus from teacher to student is reflected in *Negotiating the Curriculum: Educating for the 21st Century.* Teachers should help their students become engaged and interested in what they are learning; not just ask questions to discover what students know (Boomer, Lester, Onore, & Cook, 1992, pp. 13–16).

Ideally, teachers across the curriculum plan together for writing instruction. All the teachers, for the benefit of students, should agree on approaches to teaching writing and on evaluation standards. The writing process provides a uniform approach to writing in all subjects. Using levels of writing in every subject, as will be explained in Chapter 3, provides common teacher expectations for students. When teachers disagree on expectations and evaluate student writing differently, students become confused and even angry. They have a right to be because, rather than evaluation reflecting the purpose of writing, it depends on the personality of the teacher. Students do not become better writers under such circumstances. Writing across the entire curriculum needs to have a coherent design so that teachers and students have a common understanding of writing to learn.

Andrea Lunsford calls on teachers to create a "new scene for writing," one that "challenges divisions between disciplines, genres, and media" (1993, p. 73). The divisions between speaking, writing, reading, and listening no longer hold, and our teaching should reflect on the quality of the experiences we provide for our students (Lunsford, 1993, p. 74). The wholeness of such an approach creates a classroom where our teaching can more closely match the way we humans live and learn.

Summary

Writing serves many purposes both in and outside of school. The types of writing used in schools need to be appropriate for students' developmental stages and closely reflect real-life purposes. The types of writing—expressive, transactional, poetic—are based on speech theories. Students need to do expressive writing throughout school to remain involved with writing activities. A supportive classroom environment is essential for optimal learning. Every class includes students with a variety of learning styles, and teachers need to use several teaching approaches to accommodate them. Middle school students are at a different stage, developmentally and socially, than high school students, and teachers need to take these differences into account to facilitate learning for this age group. Although disciplines have unique writing requirements, if all the teachers in the building use the writing process and agree on evaluation levels, much of what is learned in one subject is transferable to other subjects.

Discussion Questions

1. How does writing help students learn in your discipline?
2. What are the connections between writing in school and writing outside of school?
3. How might these connections be strengthened? Should they be?
4. What do types of writing have to do with developmental stages of adolescents?
5. How can teachers involve students more in writing activities?
6. What determines classroom environment? What factors are beyond a teacher's control?

Suggested Activities

1. Using reading or nonprint material from your discipline, design a writing assignment for high school seniors. Rewrite it for seventh-graders.
2. Describe an expressive writing assignment based on an area related to your discipline.
3. Based on your own experience, list all the steps needed to write an informational paper. What do you need to know to be successful at each step? Be as detailed as possible.
4. Design an assignment that teaches students how to succeed at one of the steps in Activity #3.
5. In groups, design the ideal classroom. Include seating arrangement, colors, and objects, as well as describing teacher behavior.
6. Discover your own learning preferences by completing an assessment instrument at a career guidance center.

References

Applebee, Arthur N. *Writing in the Secondary School*. Urbana, IL: National Council of Teachers of English, 1981.

Applebee, Arthur N., Judith A. Langer, & Ina V. S. Mullis. *The Writing Report Card*. Princeton, NJ: Educational Testing Service, 1986.

Arnold, John. "A Responsive Curriculum for Emerging Adolescents." *Middle School Journal*, May 1985, pp. 1–6.

Bacon, Charles S., & Barbara J. Thayer-Bacon. "Real Talk: Enhancing Critical Thinking Skills through Conversation in the Classroom." *The Clearing House*, January–February 1993, p. 181–184.

Boomer, Garth, Nancy Lester, Cynthia Onore, & Jon Cook, eds. *Negotiating the Curriculum: Educating for the 21st Century*. London: Falmer Press, 1992.

Britton, James, Tony Burgess, Nancy Martin, Alex McLeod, & Harold Rosen. *The Development of Writing Abilities* (pp. 11–18). London: Macmillan, 1975.

Chiras, Daniel D. "Teaching Critical Thinking Skills in the Biology and Environment Science Classrooms." *The American Biology Teacher, 54*, 1992, pp. 464–468.

Davis, Barbara H., Gene E. Rooze, & Mary K. Tallent Runnels. "Writing-to-Learn in Elementary Social Studies." *Social Education, 56*(7), 1992, pp. 393–397.

Dixon, John. *Growth through English*. London: Oxford University Press, 1967.

Doney, Lloyd D., Noreen E. Lephardt, & James P. Trebby. "Developing Critical Thinking Skills in Accounting Students." *Journal of Education for Business*, May–June 1993, pp. 297–300.

Ernst, Karen. "Writing Pictures, Painting Words: Writing in an Artist's Workshop." *Language Arts, 71*, 1994, pp. 44–52.

Fortescue, Chelsea M. "Using Oral and Written Language to Increase Understanding of Math Concepts." *Language Arts, 71*, December 1994, pp. 576–580.

Fulwiler, Toby. *Teaching with Writing*. Upper Montclair, NJ: Boynton/Cook, 1987.

Freedman, Robin Lee Harris. "Writing, Students' Portfolios, and Authentic Assessment in Science." *Portfolio News*, Winter 1993, pp. 6–11.

Gere, Anne Ruggles, ed. *Roots in the Sawdust*. Urbana, IL: National Council of Teachers of English, 1985.

Hymes, Dell. "Models of the Interaction of Language and Social Life." In John J. Gumperz & Dell Hymes, eds., *Directions in Sociolinguistics*, pp. 35–71. New York: Holt, Rinehart & Winston, 1972.

Langer, Judith A., & Applebee, Arthur N. *How Writing Shapes Thinking*. Urbana, IL: National Council of Teachers of English, 1978.

Lunsford, Andrea A. "Intellectual Property, Concepts of Selfhood, and the Teaching of Writing." *The Writing Instructor,* Winter 1993, pp. 67–77.

Marzano, Robert J. "How Classroom Teachers Approach the Teaching of Thinking." *Theory into Practice* (Ohio State University), *32(3),* Summer 1993, pp. 154–160.

Moffett, James. *Teaching the Universe of Discourse.* Boston: Houghton Mifflin, 1968.

Moore, Randy. "Writing to Learn Biology." *Journal of College Science Teaching,* March–April 1994, pp. 289–295.

Murdick, William, & Richard Grinstead. "Art, Writing, and Politics." *Art Education,* September 1992, pp. 58–65.

National Association of Secondary School Principals. "On the Threshold of Adolescence." Reston: VA: NASSP, 1983.

Nelson, Laura. "Critical Thinking about Critical Thinking." *Teaching Forum, 10*(1), April 1989.

Prawat, Richard. "Teachers' Beliefs about Teaching and Learning: A Constructivist Perspective." *American Journal of Education,* May 1992, pp. 354–395.

Rief, Linda. *Seeking Diversity.* Portsmouth, NH: Heinemann, 1992.

Sapir, Edward. *Culture, Language & Personality.* Berkeley: University of California Press, 1961.

Self, Judy. "The Picture of Writing to Learn." *Plain Talk,* Virginia Department of Education, 1987, pp. 9–20.

Stout, Candace Jesse. "The Dialogue Journal: A Forum for Critical Consideration." *Studies in Art Education, 35*(1), 1993, pp. 34–44.

Tchudi, Stephen N., & Joanne Yates. *Teaching Writing in the Content Areas: High School.* Washington, DC: National Educational Association, 1983.

Vygotsky, Lev Semenovich. *Thought and Language.* Cambridge, MA: MIT Press, 1962.

Wilhoit, Stephen. "Critical Thinking and the Thematic Writing Course." *The Writing Instructor,* Spring–Summer 1993, pp. 125–133.

Winchell, Dick, & Dana Elder. "Writing in the Geography Curriculum." *Journal of Geography,* November–December 1994, pp. 273–276.

2

WRITING AS A PROCESS

People like to write. The desire to express is relentless. People want others to know what they hold to be truthful. They need the sense of authority that goes with authorship. They need to detach themselves from experience and examine it by writing. Then they need to share what they have discovered through writing.
—*DONALD H. GRAVES, 1984, P. 62.*

Prereading Questions

1. How did you learn to write?
2. What part of writing a paper is the most difficult for you?
3. What types of writing do you like the best?
4. In your middle and high school, what writing was required in subjects other than English?
5. What do you think will be the most difficult part of incorporating writing in your content area?

Introduction

Describing writing as a process suggests that writing can and should be taught throughout the time writers are composing. Too often, however, the teaching of writing takes place only after an assignment is evaluated. By carefully pointing out all the errors students make, teachers hope and expect that the writing will improve. But this negative emphasis rarely works. Learning is much easier when learners are praised for what they are doing right. If we concentrate on what we do wrong, whether we are learning to ski, bowl, write, or play an instrument, we tend to repeat our mistakes and to become discouraged.

Suggestions for improvement based on what we did right make learning easier and more successful.

Background

Traditionally, writing instruction has not followed this approach. Teachers generally ask students to write by providing the assignment and a date when the assignment is due. When the students' work is handed in, teachers note every error, shake their heads over the poor writing, and then give another assignment in the hope that students will read the comments and their writing will improve. The focus is on the product, not on the process by which students create that product. Rarely does the writing improve, especially for students who have difficulty with writing. They do not know what area or skill to work on first when their paper is covered with negative comments. Also, the problems with their writing may lie in generating ideas or even choosing an appropriate topic rather than in superficial errors. In addition, students, taught in this way, as a rule, come to dislike writing, at least school writing.

This situation has bothered educators for years, but not until a 1966 conference at Dartmouth College did the teaching of writing as a process begin to become a reality. Fifty participants from Britain and America emphasized personal growth in writing and advocated moving away from a sole concern with product to looking at how students' writing could improve during the time they were composing. In the years since then, educators have explored ways to use the process approach in classrooms.

The Writing Process

Using a process approach for teaching composition means that writers receive help and guidance from the time they begin to think about what they are going to write until the assignment is considered finished. The process is described as stages: discovering, drafting, revising, editing, and in some situations proofreading and publishing. However, the writing process is not a series of discrete steps leading to a finished product. Rather, the process is recursive as writers move back and forth among discovering, drafting, and revising.

Educators have looked for a linear approach to writing—that is, a sequence of steps inexperienced writers could follow to achieve proficiency in writing. But writing does not fall into a step-by-step structure; it requires a wide range of skills depending on the purpose for the writing and what the writer knows. With the recursive model, a writer begins with discovering, then circles back periodically while composing to provide experience with earlier approaches (Provett & Gill, 1986, p. 4).

For example, a writer uses discovery activities to define a topic, explore what he or she already knows about the topic, and brainstorm about how the writing will take shape. Then, after beginning to compose the paper, the writer may return to more discovery activities to rethink what to write and explore other directions. This recursive cycle can occur between any two stages. When revising, a writer may return, not only to drafting, but even back to discovery for more exploratory composing ideas. Throughout the process, writers move back and forth among stages as the writing demands. The emphasis remains on learning *while* composing, not after the writing is completed. A graphic illustration of the recursive nature of the writing process is shown in Figure 2–1.

To help students visualize the abstract idea of a process of writing, Golden et al. (1994) suggest an analogy with the sketches artists use as they compose their finished work of art. They based their work on the approach that Mina Shaughnessy developed working with basic writers. The students analyzed groups of pictures that encouraged generalization (Shaughnessy, 1977, p. 246). Golden et al. had students examine artists' early sketches of well-known works of art. Students could actually see the abstract concept forming into a concrete representation. The sketches served the same purpose as discovering activities and early drafts. The sketches showed how the artists added more details while the basic organization remained the same. Comparing this process to writing, students could see how they can "add new details to existing elements of a composition, enabling the whole composition to grow in a unified and harmonious way" (Golden et al., 1994, p. 199).

Stages of the Writing Process

Discovery

The discovery stage is the most important part of the composing process. During this period writers explore topics, discover what they already know (prior knowledge), think about what they need to find out, and try out different approaches. To improve at anything, we need to practice. Yet writing in school has allowed little if any time for learning how to write. If teachers taught music as they do writing, students would receive a musical score, the teachers would explain how it should sound, and students would then be expected to play it with some expertise. If students made mistakes, these would be identified; then the teacher would give out a different musical score and the procedure would begin again.

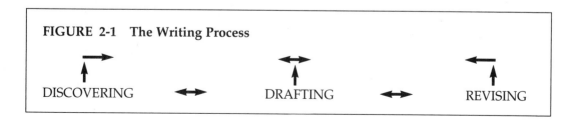

FIGURE 2-1   The Writing Process

DISCOVERING   DRAFTING   REVISING

Sounds ridiculous, doesn't it? The discovery stage provides the practice time students need to improve the content of their writing.

Often, when people think about improving their writing, they are referring to punctuation, spelling, and grammar. Although there is a stage in the writing process when these become important, the discovery stage focuses on different skills. One of the major strengths of teaching writing as a process is the focus on what the writer has to say and how it is expressed. A writer may use correct mechanical skills, but if the writing is boring, lifeless, trivial, or uninformed, it is poor writing. Professor Ken Macrorie coined the word *Engfish* to describe "the phony, pretentious language of the schools" (1980, p. 11). Engfish happens when all the teacher's attention to student writing is focused on mechanics rather than on meaning. To receive a good grade, then, students must focus on surface appearances: spelling, punctuation, format, and neatness. The problem is that correct mechanics do not ensure that the content of the paper is well-informed, interesting writing. Discovery activities shift the attention to the beginning of the writing process and to what students have to say.

The discovery stage covers many activities. All are informal, and many do not involve actual writing. Of all the possible activities, *talking* is the most important. Talking helps us to understand, to figure things out. Have you ever had the experience of asking a question and then, in the process of explaining what it is you don't understand, realizing that you have answered your own question? Thinking out loud is a good strategy for clarifying our thoughts, and teachers need to plan for this to happen in the classroom. Small-group discussions allow students to attempt to clarify their own thinking and to hear what others know about a particular topic. The following example illustrates how classroom talk becomes part of the learning process.

Before students begin a unit on photosynthesis, they meet in groups and talk about what they believe photosynthesis is, what the unit will cover, and what they already know about the topic. Following the discussion, they jot down a summary of the discussion in their journal. When students have the opportunity to talk about a topic before actually studying it, they become actively involved right from the beginning. Later, when students have finished reading a related assignment in the textbook, they answer four or five questions provided by the teacher—not simple recall questions, but ones that require interpretation and synthesis. Rather than turn in the work, students meet in small groups again and discuss their answers. The opportunities to talk about their reading help them clarify confusions and misunderstandings. The summaries of the discussions help the teacher tailor the lectures for the students. This example from science illustrates how talk becomes an integral part of the learning process, but talk is important in every subject. Throughout this book, student talk is included in descriptions of classroom activities.

Discovery activities also include writing as a way of generating ideas. Mapping or webbing, free writing or brainstorming, outlining, and creative dramatics are all examples of discovery writing.

Brainstorming (or Free Writing)

The object of brainstorming is to gather all one's thoughts about a subject. For instance, if students are planning to write a report on a particular topic, they begin by writing the topic at the top of a page. Then, as quickly as possible, they write down everything they know about the topic, not in any order but just as the thoughts come to mind. The point is to cover as much of the page as possible in a limited amount of time.

Students might think of this as storming around their brain, quickly searching out knowledge and recording it with no regard for any writing conventions. When the brainstorming session is completed, students read the material over and circle phrases and words that are appropriate for the report. Because the writing is done quickly with no reflection, some thoughts will go off on a tangent. The term *free* means that the writer is free to write anything that comes to mind. Fast writing can tap into ideas that more thoughtful, slower writing would never uncover. Also, the writer is free from any constraints imposed by mechanics or spelling. Following free writing, students read their jottings over and circle ideas they want to expand. An example of a free write or brainstorming that was done for a science class is shown in Figure 2–2.

FIGURE 2-2   Brainstorming

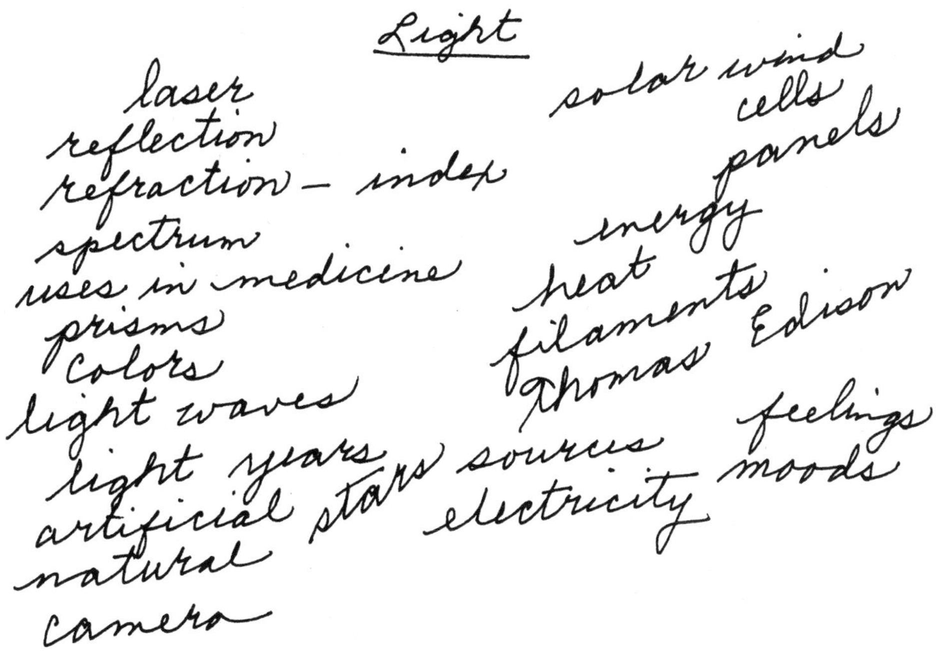

Mapping (Clustering or Webbing)

Gabriele Lusser Rico has developed many ways of clustering ideas as a way of getting thoughts down on paper. She explains that a writer needs to be immersed in the discovering process. Clustering "not only frees your expressive power but also helps you discover what you have to say, encouraging a flow instead of a mere trickle" (1983, p. 27). She describes clustering as a technique of "natural writing" where a "nucleus or short phrase acts as the stimulus for recording all the associations that spring to mind in a very brief period of time" (Rico, 1983, p. 30). Figure 2–3 illustrates what a student, Cassie Scharber, wrote for the word *happiness*.

For mapping, students write their topic in the middle of a sheet of paper and then circle it. The topic could be a single word or a phrase. Concentrating on the topic for a few seconds, they then write a word or phrase the topic makes them think of. They repeat this until they have written as much as they can think of. Figure 2–4 shows an example from science. When the map or web is completed, the writer organizes it into a general outline to use when beginning the actual report.

FIGURE 2-3   Clustering

FIGURE 2-4   Mapping

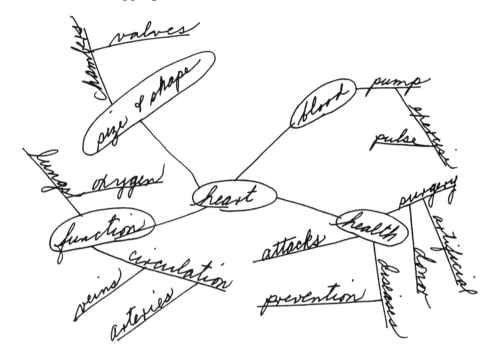

Mapping can be used for any subject and for a variety of writing assignments. Figure 2–5 illustrates a map a student, Jenna Sims, wrote to help her understand how the ideas in a novel she had read are associated and connected.

Outlining

In the past, outlining was the only prewriting activity students did. Because of the inflexibility with which teachers used outlining, it is generally not recognized as helpful in the writing process. If it is approached as a discovery activity, however, some students find outlining helpful. Teachers must keep in mind the variety of learning styles present in their classrooms, and this more organized approach to mapping benefits students who have trouble with free writing or mapping. Without using Roman numerals or any particular method of numbering, students write out the major points they want to cover. Then they jot down the topics that fall under these main ideas. This is called a *working outline* to emphasize that it changes as the writing takes shape. Figure 2–6 is an illustration of an informal outline.

Some writers use outlining not as a means of planning what to write about but as a way of organizing their first drafting attempts. The outlining serves as an intermediate step before revision. Ginny McBride, who wrote the following example, finds outlining helpful only after she has written a first draft. She says, "I

FIGURE 2-5   Mapping

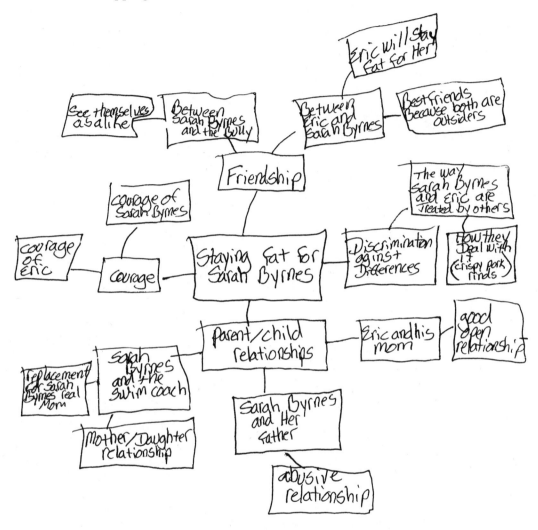

can't outline until I see what I'm going to say." The example in Figure 2–7 shows first the writer's draft, then the subsequent outline.

As McBride wrote the outline, she added and deleted information. Her next step is to write another draft based on her organization. Also, she will find additional information to support her points.

Creative Dramatics

Creative dramatics is another discovery activity useful for clarifying thinking and providing ideas for writing. In English class, students might present informal

FIGURE 2-6   An Informal Outline

Wisconsin

```
Geography
  Rivers & lakes
    tourist industry
      fishing
      hunting
  Great Lakes
  land features
    glaciers
    rocks

Industries
  logging
  fishing
  farming
    dairy

History
  Native Americans
    trading posts
  explorers
    forts
  early settlements

Cultures
  German
  Native Americans
  Scandinavians
  Hmong
```

skits in which characters discuss the motivations and consequences of actions in a story. Acting out impromptu skits with no prepared script helps students think through a writing assignment or simply come to a better understanding of their reading. As with other discovery techniques, creative dramatics may lead to other writing assignments or may not develop any further after serving its purpose of helping students learn.

An example of using creative dramatics in English as an activity to provide practice rather than leading directly into a writing assignment is the use of impromptu skits that develop skill in writing dialogue. The students work in groups of four or five. Each group receives a bag of props collected by the teacher. A bag

FIGURE 2-7   A First Draft

How the tourist industry brings income to northern Minn.

The income from tourism provides a living for many people - resort owners, cafe and restaurant owners and workers, cooks, wait people etc. - dock boys, fishing guides, even the fish hatcheries. - Lots of college students hope for summer jobs at resorts. Schools in Minnesota. The school year in Minnesota should be between Labor Day and Memorial Day to accomodate these students. Bad weather (rain and cool temps) also are part of it. Near my home is a pie shop/souvenier shop which is only open for 3 months each summer - a bad tourist season means a great deal of difference to their income. Bait shops need a large volume of tourists stopping by each day. What would be some good ways to increase business opportunities? Advertising on radio, tv, special "vacation" newspapers? Is it worthwhile to advertise nation-wide at "boat and sport shows" The manufacturing of boats, fishing rolds, reels, lures etc. also are determined by the number of people who come.

The outline written following the draft:

How the Tourist Industry Brings Income to Northern Minnesota
     1. All the types of business affected
        Resorts
        Campgrounds
        State Parks
        Eating establishments
        Fishing related works
        And all the people who work at the above
     2. How weather affects total income
     3. Advertising
        tv, radio, newspaper
        boat and sport shows
        word of mouth

might include a pair of safety glasses, a hammer, several pieces of hard candy, a banana, an empty ring box, and a Chinese fan. Each group has only twenty minutes or less to think up a skit using *every* prop in the bag. Another version of this activity is to have identical props for each group. The groups of students perform the skits with the other students as the audience. After the students present the skits, the class discusses how the dialogue carried the plot along and developed the characterization.

Although English provides more opportunities for using creative dramatics than other subjects do, the social sciences also are appropriate areas for this type of discovery activity. Role playing helps students understand differing points of view.

The following activity illustrates the use of creative dramatics in social studies. After a class has read and discussed an environmental issue concerning mining or lumbering in an area, the teacher hands out slips of paper assigning various roles: an employee of the Department of Natural Resources, a laid-off worker, a company administrator, a taxpayer in the local community, an environmentalist, a scientist, and a sport hunter. These people are taking part in an open forum to discuss whether or not the mine should open or the lumbering take place. The rest of the class play the parts of news media people who are free to ask questions of the participants after the discussion.

Opportunities for discussions on issues help students understand that few, if any, problems or current events have only two sides. The multidimensional characteristics of real-life problems call for critical thinking and sensitivity to others' points of view. Talking and arguing during role playing help students write more detailed and thoughtful papers. The more discussion activities require active participation from students, the better they engage students as active learners.

Discovery activities are an essential part of the writing process, but they are the part most often slighted. Arthur Applebee found, on the basis of many observational studies, that the time teachers spend on any activity prior to the drafting stage averaged just over three minutes (1981, p. 74). This includes introducing the topic, handing out copies, and answering questions about when the assignment is due and what the writing should look like. No matter how carefully teachers explain an assignment, unless students have the time to explore a topic through reading, writing, thinking, and talking, their writing will not improve.

In addition to increasing the time spent on discovery activities, teachers need to give students a variety of activities from which to choose because of the different learning styles represented in the classrooms. Some writers find a particular activity helpful, while others do not. For this reason, it is important to suggest two or three discovery activities to the class and then let students decide which ones they want to use.

Drafting

Drafting is an ongoing process, interspersed with sharing the writing with others, collecting information, thinking about the topic, and returning to discovery activities for fresh ideas and ways to organize what the writer wants to say. Teachers must help students realize that all writing is an evolving process. Peter Elbow describes the process as one that "is not so much like filling a basin or pool once, but rather getting water to keep flowing through till finally it runs clear" (1973, p. 28). We write drafts, not finished papers; therefore, a polished paper has multiple drafts.

A first draft is a messy business because writers are pulling ideas together, trying out organizations, and concentrating only on the major part of the paper. Rarely does a first draft include an introduction or an opening line. In fact, introductions make the most sense and are the most effective if they are written after the paper is completed. Trying to think of that first line to write can be an enormous stumbling block. Writers should begin writing what they know they want to say on the basis of the discovery activities. A good starting point is for a writer to ask, "What do I know?" and "What do I need to find out?"

This is not the time to worry about mechanics and spelling. Those become important in a later draft. When a writer is concentrating on what to write, worrying about mechanics and spelling gets in the way of thinking. Teachers should help students realize that worrying about correctness in a first draft interferes with successful writing.

Teachers should always refer to the writing as *drafting* or *producing drafts*. When teachers ask a student if he or she is working on a second or third draft, they are emphasizing the notion of multiple drafts. When the assignment is turned in, it is called a *final draft* because no paper is ever really finished. Usually, we stop working on a paper because of a due date, and we hope it is sufficiently well done to satisfy oneself and the teacher. Given more time, however, the paper could be improved. This is true in real-world writing as well as in school.

An important point to make here is that all writing does not go through every stage of the writing process. Some assignments require several drafts, but other assignments do not require extensive revisions. The purpose and audience for the writing determines the amount of revision and editing. The next chapter on writing levels examines the roles of purpose and audience in writing.

Revising

Revising is probably the most difficult part of writing, both to teach and to learn. The need to revise is not always clear to the student writer. Using revision as one part of the writing process helps put it in perspective. The first writing, as described, is thinking and talking transferred to written form with little regard for writing conventions. Using this approach leads to writing that is interesting and rich in detail. If anyone but the writer is to read and understand it, however, revision must take place.

Revising and editing are two different events. Many pieces of writing will be revised, but final editing is not always necessary; it depends on the intended audience. Revision may require writers to "add new material to develop ideas, to delete distracting material, and to reorganize the material into a more effective logical arrangement" (Golden et al., 1994, p. 205). Revising means looking at organization, word choice, main points, support for main ideas, examples, connections between ideas, and a clear focus. Is what the writer said understandable, believable, and interesting? There is no reason to edit for punctuation, spelling, and other superficial writing conventions if the writing is not meant for a wider audience. If revising and editing are not separated, it is the revising that is slighted because it is more difficult for both author and reader to do. Yet, without revising, the editing alone will not improve a piece of writing.

Revising Begins with the Writer

Revision always begins with the writer. The most important reason is that the writer is the one responsible. That may sound like an obvious statement, but students sometimes seem genuinely puzzled about their own writing and have no sense of ownership. This feeling comes about in part because they are only writing because the teacher told them to do so. Using the writing process, and in particular the discovery activities, helps to eliminate this reaction. Teachers can help, too, by asking what the writer thinks of the paper. It is frustrating when a student asks, "Is this what you wanted?" or "Is this right?" We want students to develop a greater sense of responsibility for their own learning. One way to achieve this is to ask students if they like what they have written and if they think it could be improved.

One technique that helps all writers is to read their papers aloud to themselves. Actually hearing the words helps writers to catch redundancies and omissions. Also, we may hear problems in organization: If the writing does not read easily, we may realize the thoughts are not in the right order. If students do not read their own papers first before reading to others, they spend a lot of time explaining to their response group what they "meant to say." Writers who come to the groups prepared because they have read their own work to themselves first are in an excellent position to receive the help they need. The first step in the revision process, then, is for writers to read their papers aloud to themselves.

Another technique that helps writers with revision is to have them read only their first and last paragraphs. Do these explain what the paper is about and how it was developed? Would a reader understand what the writer was attempting to accomplish in the paper?

Also, a writer can write a short summary of the paper. This helps to check for weakness in the argument or description. Writing an outline when the paper is considered finished helps to check for gaps in detail and supporting points.

Response Groups

When writers feel ready or the teacher establishes a time, students meet with a peer response group. The groups are quite large, with five or six members, so that each writer has the benefit of hearing what several people think of the paper. The groups are formed in a variety of ways. Students may select on their own whom they want to work with, or the groups can be formed by students counting off, or the teacher may want to decide on group membership. Each method has pros and cons. The teacher might decide on group membership by mixing ability levels or by combining quieter students with more outgoing ones. If students always choose group members, some students may feel left out or cliques may become a problem. But if only teachers choose group members, students may resent not having the freedom to decide whom they can work with. Using a variety of methods gives students opportunities to get to know each other better while allowing them to work with good friends on occasion.

Students come to the response groups with a complete first draft. Each writer, in turn, reads his or her paper aloud to the others. There are two reasons to have the writer read the paper to the others. The more important one is that if others actually read the paper, the emphasis is on surface elements. It is difficult, if not impossible, to read a paper and not notice misspellings and incorrect punctuation. At this point in the writing process, writing conventions are not an issue and actually get in the way of responding to the context (what the writer is telling the reader). All the attention needs to focus on what the paper is about, not on writing conventions.

The second reason for reading the paper is that it may be impossible for others to read. Although it depends somewhat on the availability of computers, most rough drafts are written by hand, which makes them difficult to follow. Writers may use arrows to insert additional information, scratch out unwanted words, or use unconventional spelling and abbreviations.

Responding to someone's writing in a helpful way is not easy. Students find it helpful if a teacher models the process for the class before response groups are used for the first time. In addition, the sheets on which students write responses give structure to the group work. Response sheets vary somewhat depending on the subject of the writing, but most ask the same type of questions. Figure 2–8 illustrates a response sheet for a social studies assignment. Response sheets must reflect the purpose of the assignment. If the purpose is to write an informational report, then response questions focus on the amount of information, details, clear explanations, and perhaps comparisons. If the purpose is to explain what happens in a series of experiments or observations, than the questions would be about sequence, descriptions, results, and precise words.

Not all response sheets are as detailed as the one in Figure 2–8. Often it is more appropriate to have students use a shorter response sheet, but one that still requires them to give a thoughtful response. Figure 2–9 illustrates one used by Dennis Crowe, a high school teacher. He has the writer attach this to the final draft.

How Response Groups Work

The students meet in their response groups during class time. They need a full class period because of the size of the groups, and teachers may have to adjust the number of students in a group to the length of time a class meets. One at a time, students read their papers to the others. Because they do not see the paper, the others must listen carefully. They may jot down notes about what they want to mention when the author is finished reading. The author reads the paper through

FIGURE 2-8   Response Sheet

Introduction

1. In what ways does the intro create interest for readers?

2. How could the thesis make a stronger statement?

Body of the paper

3. What major questions does the paper answer?

4. How could the main questions and the intro be more closely connected?

5. How could the writer support the questions better?

6. Where do references seem awkward and not smoothly incorporated into the text?

7. What points seem unclear or incomplete?

Conclusion

8. How does the conclusion pull all the pieces together?

9. How could it make a stronger, more thoughtful statement?

In general   What area needs the most revision?

with no interruptions. Once through, the group members respond, often asking to have a section or a sentence read again. The writer and other group members talk about the paper, with everyone contributing something.

Generally the comments begin with positive and general remarks, a good way to make the writer comfortable. Students know, however, that their task is to help each other improve their writing, so they start to talk about ways to accomplish that. During the teacher's modeling, students learn to ask questions about the writing rather than make statements. Rather than say, "I don't get what you mean," a student asks, "What happened after you told her?" or "Why did the general decide that?" The more specific the questions are, the more helpful they are to the writer. During this discussion or following it, students fill out a response sheet for the writer. The process continues until everyone in the group has read his or her paper. At the conclusion of the class, each student has suggestions to read over and consider for revisions. No one is required to use the suggestions offered. Each writer maintains responsibility for the paper. Sometimes the

---

FIGURE 2-9   A Shorter Response Sheet

Name of Reader _____

Dear Reader: Peer evaluation is a mutual assistance activity. Please write down specific questions you have concerning the writing which you have just read. Write 3 questions. Each question should begin with one of the following words:

Who, what, where, when, why, how

Thank you.

1._____

_____

2._____

_____

3._____

_____

---

responses give conflicting advice, and it is up to the writer to decide what to do. Response groups improve the quality of student writing tremendously.

Editing

Few writing assignments require an editing stage. Editing and proofreading are necessary only when the audience is wider than the classroom, usually when the writing is to be published. Criteria for deciding when editing is appropriate are explained in the next chapter. When editing is required, it follows the revising stage as a separate step. As mentioned earlier, revision needs to remain apart from attention to mechanics.

Following the response group meeting, students revise their papers. They may meet with the group again or with one or two members to receive further responses. Once writers are satisfied with their own work, they produce a clean copy. For editing work, students meet in pairs. Generally, they are free to choose their own partners. They exchange papers and read each other's papers carefully, looking for punctuation, spelling, word choice, grammar, run-on sentences, and sentence fragments. As in the revising stage, what they pay attention to in editing depends somewhat on the purpose of the writing. If the paper includes documented sources, the editor must check for introduction to the borrowed material, the dates of the sources, and the pages cited. Editing guidelines are helpful, especially when students have difficulty with particular areas. The editing guidelines are used for reminders and, like response sheets, vary according to the type of writing. An example of an editing guideline is illustrated in Figure 2–10.

Usually students make notes on each other's papers, although they should always ask permission first. Questions come up about writing conventions, and this is when the handbooks come into use. Students also ask each other for help with punctuation and word use; only in cases when a decision seems impossible to reach should students involve the teacher. Rather than supply an immediate answer, however, the teacher and the student together check the handbook. Frequently, the problem is that students cannot find the appropriate reference in the handbook. Looking it up together helps students learn how to find answers so that another time they can locate the information themselves. Whatever subject one teaches, grammar handbooks and dictionaries need to be available in the classrooms. Students might ask two or three students to look their work over because, when the next step is publishing, the writer wants an error-free paper.

FIGURE 2-10   An Editing Guide

Word Usage

Where do redundancies occur?

Where are words too general?

Look specifically for subject-verb agreement.

Suggest changes for clichés.

Punctuation

Ask the writer what in particular you should check.

Check for run-on sentences.

Where might semicolons be appropriate?

If the paper includes references, use a style guide to assure correct punctuation.

Spelling

Read slowly to catch errors. If there is any doubt, check it out.

Transitions

Where might additional transitions help create a smoother and more cohesive paper?

Publishing

Publishing is an important part of the writing process when it is used sparingly. Most of the writing we and our students do is not for publication. Writing for learning is largely not for publication. Occasionally, a situation comes up in which students see the importance of their writing reaching a wider audience. For example, an idea to send letters to newspapers to explain or argue a contemporary issue can develop out of a class discussion, or students may decide to write letters for information they need for reports. Teachers may design assignments that depend on a wider audience: contests, school publications, class anthologies.

Published writing should be free from all errors. A student must write a polished final draft, which takes a great deal of time. When students know their work will be read by a wider audience, they are motivated to do the necessary revising, editing, and polishing; but the time needed for this cuts down on time for a variety of other writing activities. Although publishing is a worthwhile and appropriate experience, we have to make sure that it does not interfere with developing fluency and interest for our students.

Teacher Help

Teachers are part of the entire writing process, but they also need to know when to stand back. Students most often require teacher help in the discovery and early drafting stages. Teacher-provided questions are helpful when one is searching for ideas. When the papers reach the revising and editing stage, writers are much better off relying on their peers than on teachers. We want to enable student writers to write well without teacher help; therefore, our goal is to provide ways for them to help themselves, not to do the work for them. Our help is more in guiding them rather than telling them. English teachers, in particular, are apt to overhelp by collecting rough drafts and making or suggesting changes for the writer. Doing this takes responsibility for the writing away from the student. Unless students have a sense of responsibility or ownership, their writing does not improve. Our job, then, is to set up opportunities for students to receive help from each other and to provide instruction when necessary. The more a teacher controls the writing, the more the students will write to please the teacher and not themselves. Consequently, their writing loses vitality and the individual flair that only the writer can provide.

All the ideas and assignments presented in this textbook follow the belief that the teaching of writing happens while students are in the process of writing, not after an assignment is handed in to the teacher. Also, the integration of writing and learning involves the students most when presented as an ongoing process.

Summary

The way writing is taught in schools has changed from an emphasis on the product to active participation of students in a process of thinking, writing, and learning. The writing process includes discovery, drafting, revising, editing, and publishing. The stages are recursive; that is, writers move back and forth among them.

In the discovery stage, writers search for ideas and focus. Although many activities contribute to discovery, talking is the most important one. Students need reading, writing, thinking, and talking to improve their writing.

During drafting, writers receive help with revision from their classmates and produce many drafts. Revision concentrates on organization, word choice, examples, focus, and connections. Revision always begins with the writer and only then involves response groups.

Editing is important only when a wider audience calls for conventional forms of written language. During editing, students look at punctuation, spelling, word choice, grammar, and sentence structure. Publishing may follow the editing work if the writing is intended for a wide audience.

Discussion Questions

1. Discuss negative versus positive comments in the process of learning something. Use your own experiences as examples.
2. What is meant by *recursive* in the context of the writing process? In what ways do you use the stages in your own writing?
3. When you have "writer's block," what do you do?
4. How do you involve your friends when you are writing a paper?
5. Under what circumstances would one revise but not edit? Draft but not revise?

Suggested Activities

1. Choose a writing assignment you had difficulty with and design discovery activities that could have helped you.
2. Write a assignment that is appropriate for middle or high school students, perhaps one you enjoyed doing at that age. What discovery activities might help students get started?
3. Write a response sheet that students could use for the assignment in activity 2.
4. Write a list of at least ten writing activities students could do to increase understanding and interest in your teaching area.
5. Design a writing assignment in your content area that includes all the steps of the writing process.

References

Applebee, Arthur N. *Writing in the Secondary School.* Urbana, IL: National Council of Teachers of English, 1981.

Dixon, John. *Growth through English.* London: Oxford University Press, 1967.

Elbow, Peter. *Writing without Teachers.* London: Oxford University Press, 1973.

Gemake, Josephine, & Richard Sinatra. "Using Maps to Improve Writing." *Early Years,* November–December, 1986, pp. 52–55.

Golden, Catherine, et al. "Visualization as a Guide for Composing." *Reading and Writing: An Interdisciplinary Journal, 6,* 1994, pp. 197–214.

Graves, Donald H. *A Researcher Learns to Write.* Exeter, NH: Heinemann, 1984.

Macrorie, Ken. *Telling Writing,* 3rd ed. Rochelle Park, NJ: Hayden Book Company, 1980.

Provett, Jackie, & Kent Gill. *The Writing Process in Action.* Urbana, IL: National Council of Teachers of English, 1986.

Rico, Gabriele Lusser. *Writing the Natural Way.* Los Angeles: J. P. Tarcher, 1983.

Shaughnessy, Mina. *Errors and Expectations.* New York: Oxford University Press, 1977.

3

LEVELS OF WRITING

We begin at home with the family; and starting from this center, create ever-widening circles of social involvement. In the neighborhood we have casual and informal associations with those nearby. . . . There are also "neighborhoods" that the individual enters wherever he or she spends time—at a job, in school, or at a library. Beyond the neighborhoods of the individual is the town or city; beyond the city the county; and beyond the county, the state, country, world, and universe.
—*JAMES E. MILLER, JR. AND STEPHEN N. JUDY, 1978*

Prereading Questions

1. Is it ever O.K. to write with no or little regard for punctuation and spelling? When?
2. What kind of writing are you most comfortable with? Why?
3. What connections might exist between the way we talk and the way we write?
4. What determines how formal or "correct" our speech is?
5. When in our life might we use different levels of behavior or appearance?

Introduction

Writing is varied in purpose and form. Writing may be a note on a scrap of paper reminding oneself to buy a bottle of milk, or it could be a poem done in calligraphy. Levels of formality exist in writing as in so many other areas of our life. Writing, however, especially writing done in school, is often thought of being on one level—work that is always correctly and neatly done. On the contrary, writing has various levels of formality in school as well as in the real world. On some occasions, writing requires the most formal style; correct punctuation, grammar, word choice, and spelling are as important as the content of the piece. More often, though, the writing requires only a style that makes it easy for a reader to comprehend what the writer intends; punctuation, grammar and spelling are not major concerns. Finally, there is a more casual type of writing that might make sense to the writer alone or at best to people well acquainted with the writer and his or her way of writing. At this level, correctness in writing skills is of little or no importance.

Determining Levels

Many areas of our life are affected by the concept of differing standards. We vary our eating manners depending on where we eat and with whom. Our behavior when sitting on the floor eating pizza with friends is quite different from our behavior while eating at an upscale restaurant. Perhaps to a lesser degree, our clothing changes, too. What we wear to a fairly formal setting, where people we do not know will see us, is different from what we wear at home. We have different expectations for ourselves depending on the setting or context, or, to put it another way, the audience. Writing, too, changes with different expectations. Using differing degrees of correctness for writing in the classroom creates a reasonable context and helps students understand the purposes of different assignments.

Teachers often do not make clear distinctions for students among appropriate standards or degrees of correctness for writing. Consequently, students are confused about the expectations for each writing assignment. A teacher might explain that an assignment is only for their eyes and is intended to help them think through a concept, but still students ask if spelling, neatness, or organization matters. When a teacher does convince them that in this particular instance, the content is all they should be concerned with, they are confused when, for another assignment, they are expected to write an error-free paper. The most serious aspect of the problem is that students take no responsibility in deciding what standard should apply to the writing. They expect the teacher to tell them. Rather than continue to need piecemeal explanations, assignment by assignment, students need to understand how purpose and audience define the appropriate standards or levels.

Writing serves many purposes: to inform, to entertain, to remember, to create, to understand. Writing, too, may have a variety of audiences: oneself, teachers, classmates, unknown readers. Purposes and audiences combine in various ways to shape the way a piece of writing looks. Yet, in school, writing is often expected by teachers, parents, and even the students themselves to be always at the most formal level. Many believe that regardless of the purpose and audience, punctuation, spelling, and grammar are as important as content, if not more so. However, writing can appropriately appear informal.

We need to recognize the varieties of writing in content classes. Formal writing is only a small part of the writing students actually do. Students typically spend most class hours writing in a form that we do not grade (Lehning, 1993, p. 342). For instance, writing that is intended to help one study for an exam is probably messy and in note form, with some words circled or underlined, little punctuation, and dashes used as a means of organization. By contrast, a report or essay written for a wider audience usually requires a high degree of correctness in all the writing skills. Answers to questions, often done as homework, fall somewhere between the two extremes. The purpose for the writing and the intended audience account for the differences among the levels. All three levels are extremely important in writing to learn because each level helps us to understand in different ways.

Functions of Writing

The work of James Britton, Nancy Martin, and their colleagues in Great Britain provides the scaffolding for thinking of writing categories determined by function. Their categories—expressive, transactional, and poetic—are described by the intended audience and the purpose for the writing. In other words, what the writer hopes to achieve and who will be reading the writing determine the function. The function categories of writing relate to the levels described here. Function describes the purpose of the writing. The function category of level 1 writing is for communicating to oneself and/or close friends. In *expressive* writing, the writer also takes for granted the interest of the audience, no matter how casual or informal the style. It is close to written speech—that is, speech for an intimate audience (Martin, Medway, Smith, & D'Arcy, 1984, p. 42).

The audience for level 2 writing is a known one but broader in scope. Whereas level 1 is for a small number of close friends, level 2 needs to be understood by the members of a response group or the members of a whole class. In similar fashion, Martin describes the *transactional* category as one that does not "derive its validity from coming from a particular person" (Martin et al., 1984, p. 44). That is, the understandings must be available to a wider audience than close personal friends. Transactional writing is traditionally school writing where the personality of the writer seems of little importance and the purpose of the writing is to show what one knows, by repeating or rephrasing information a writer gained through reading or listening.

Level 3 is intended for an even wider audience, including people whom the writer may or may not know. Martin, Medway, Smith and D'Arcy describe this third category as *poetic* and describe it as an experience rather than a representation of reality (p. 45). This type of writing could be at any of the levels, but would most likely be level 1, intended only for oneself, or level 3, intended for wide distribution. The levels of writing are related to purposes for school assignments and, consequently, to evaluation of these assignments. Martin emphasizes that teachers need to discuss the function categories with students to help them understand what and whom the writing is for (1984, p. 51). The same is true for levels of writing. Without knowing the function and audience, student writers have difficulty developing their writing proficiency.

Levels of Speech

Purposes and audiences determine levels of speech, too. We need levels of speech to assure communication throughout different settings. Martin Joos in *The Five Clocks* illustrates the need for varying levels by the following story:

> Ballyhough railway station has two clocks which disagree by some six minutes. When one helpful Englishman pointed the fact out to a porter, his reply was "Faith sir, if they was to tell the same time, why would we be having two of them?" (Joos, 1961, p. 1).

We probably don't need clocks that tell different times, but the point of the story helps us to realize that different "clocks" or scales of language play important roles in communication.

Joos describes five scales of language based on the social utility of language. All of the scales are necessary and appropriate depending on the speaker's audience. To insist that only one scale is acceptable is like demanding that the "clocks of language all be set to Central Standard Time" (Joos, 1961, p. 4). All of the scales are respectable; informal speech is not inferior.

Along the same lines, the sociolinguist Dell Hymes explains a *functional classification* where the level or mode of speech is formed by the settings and activities surrounding the speech act (Hymes, 1972, p. 43). The community in which one is speaking determines the appropriate linguistic variety a speaker uses and listeners expect (p. 57). Formal language is incorrect if used in a community of well-known friends, or "insiders," as Joos describes them (p. 23).

A casual type of talking is for sharing with an audience well known to the speaker—friends and family. Characteristics of this type of speech include unfinished sentences, slang expressions, informal sentence structure, and references to shared knowledge such as former experiences, jokes, and common readings. The audience must be familiar. In my own family, whenever the weather turns cold with blowing snow, someone is sure to say, "It's not a fit night out for man or beast," a line from an old W. C. Fields movie. The result is invariably a hearty laugh because we remember the ridiculous scene of a prop person throwing snow in Fields's face. Without the context of shared knowledge, people outside the family circle would not understand. Or someone might begin a sentence and another person interrupt and answer, knowing ahead of time what the first was going to say. Communication can be so familiar it is wordless; a facial expression might be sufficient to ask a question or make a comment. Donald Rubin describes language with an intimate audience as elliptical and choppy; the rhetorical context and the intent of the message affect the language style (Rubin, 1990, p. 5). The purpose of such casual speech is to communicate to a well-known audience. Level 1 in writing compares in style to this casual speech.

To summarize, then, the three levels of writing are based on the work of James Britton, Nancy Martin, and others, as well as the work of Dell Hymes. Purpose of writing, audience, form, and function all describe the levels of writing. The levels determine the style and evaluation of writing activities.

Level 1

We use level 1 writing commonly in familiar situations—for instance, when making a list of things to do or buy. Notes to ourselves or to those we know well are at level 1. Spelling and punctuation are immaterial at this level. A grocery list posted on the refrigerator does not require correct spelling. We buy the correct vegetable if we write *carrotts,* or *carots,* or *carrots.* Abbreviations pose no problem: *oj, tp, thp, bf.* The first two might be universally known, but probably only my family or close friends know I also need toothpaste and cereal (breakfast food). We don't need to write, "Remember to buy stamps at the post office"; a note with STAMPS across it reminds us as well. For such situations, casual writing is appropriate. The purpose of level 1 includes writing to remember, to sort out thoughts, to organize, and to communicate. The audience of level one is oneself and others well known to the writer.

Many opportunities exist for level 1 writing in school situations as well as in private life. Note-taking provides the most common example, whether the notes come from reading, viewing, or listening. The purpose of writing notes is to remember, of course, but it is also to figure things out, especially when the notes are reread later. When reading notes from a variety of sources, we understand connections and see patterns more readily than when we rely on memory alone. Journals or learning logs are at level 1 as writers sort through information, ask themselves questions, and summarize what they have learned. The audience is largely only the writer, although on occasion classmates may read or listen to the writer read the journal or notes; in that case, the writer is always present to interpret or offer further explanations. First drafts are at level 1, as are all discovery activities. The first attempts at getting down on paper what one remembers and thinks about is a messy business. To break a train of thought or interrupt thinking to worry about writing skills results in mundane and stilted writing. Figure 3–1 is an example of high school student, Aaron Gordon, discovering what points he will use when writing a paper for social studies. He establishes main ideas and organization in a messy but readable and helpful fashion for his own use.

Level 2

Level 2 writing also compares to a level of speech, the type we use when talking to people we know, but not as intimate friends. Examples of audiences appropriate for level 2 include people we communicate with on a day-to-day basis—store clerks, acquaintances, teachers, and classmates. The level of speech must be understood by a wider range, so vocabulary, grammar, and delivery must follow an accepted style, although informality is acceptable as long as communication occurs.

FIGURE 3-1   Level 1 Writing

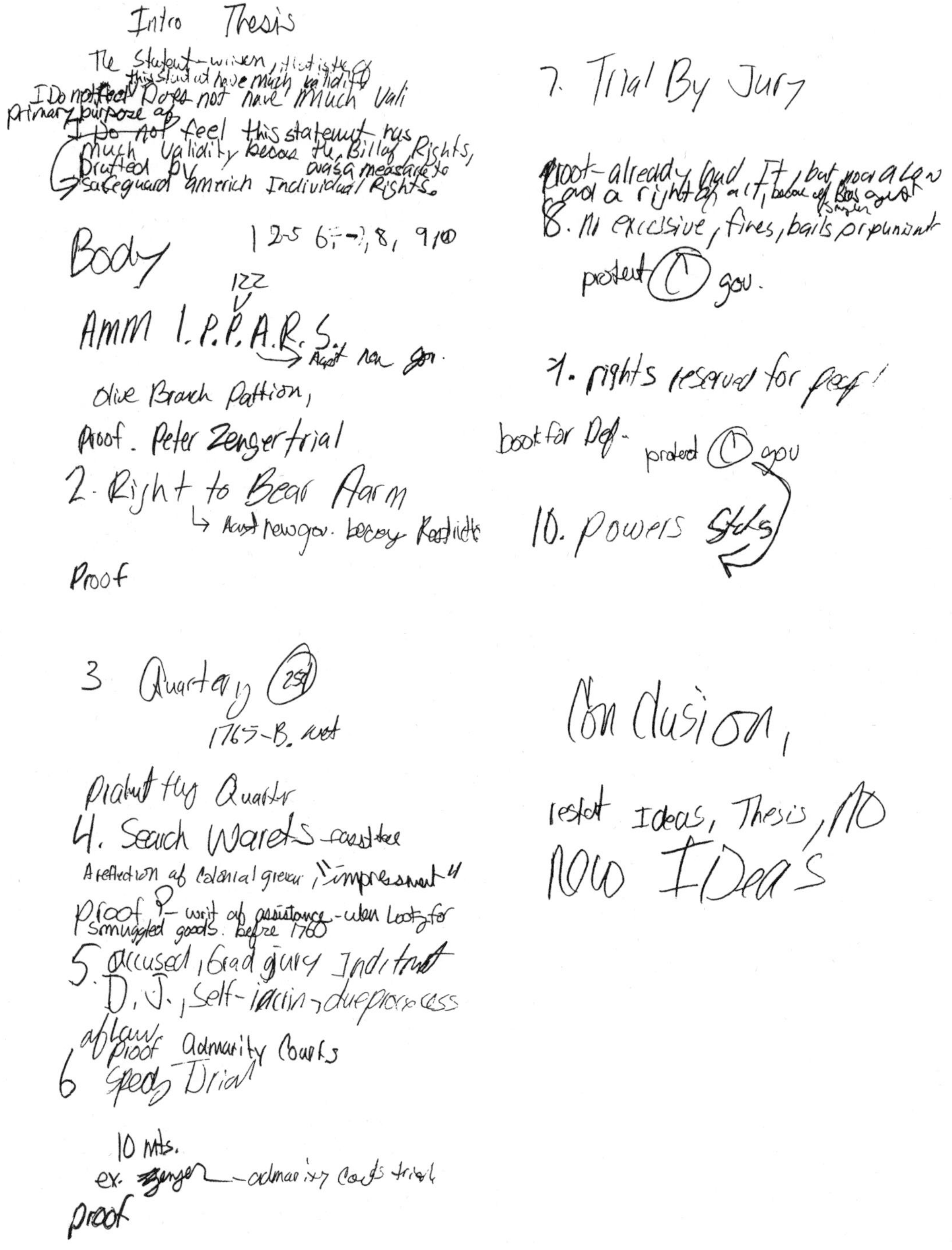

Intro   Thesis

The student-writer, that is of
this statement have much validity
I do notice Does not have much vali
primary purpose as
I do not feel this statement has
much validity becas the Bill of Rights,
Drafted by   as a measure to
safeguard americn Individual Rights.

Body   1 2-5 6, -7, 8, 9 10

Amm I. P. P. A. R. S. 1zz
                    → Agst new gov.

Olive Branch Pattion,

Proof. Peter Zenger trial

2. Right to Bear Aarm
        → Aust new gov. becay Redcoats

Proof

3   Quartery (254)
        1765~B. act

Praht thy Quarter

4. Search Warrets —

A reflection of colonial greve "impressment"

Proof ? — writ of assistance — when look for
smuggled goods. Before 1760

5. accused, Grad gury Indictmt
    D. J., self-incin, due process
        of law
        Proof. admiralty Courts
6 Speedy Trial

10 nts.
ex. Zenger — admiralty Cout trial

proof

7. Trial By Jury

Proof - already had Ft, but poor a Lew
      gave a right   in it, becoz of Bros agnst

8. No excessive, fines, bails or punisnt

    protect (I) gov.

9. rights reserved for peop!

    book for Def. — protect (I) gov

10. Powers Stats

Conclusion,

restat Ideas, Thesis, NO

NEW IDEA'S

A comparable level in writing appears in informal letter writing, notes to people outside the intimate circle of friends and family, written instructions or directions, and all situations where communication depends on well-known constructions of language. The writer usually is not present to elaborate on or explain what was meant; the writing must stand on its own for communication to take place. The following paragraph from a personal communication illustrates this level:

> Believe me—Jeff can get you the house you want, in the location you want, at the price you want. Best of all—you can trust him. You both have time—so by connecting with Jeff now—he will have time to find what you desire. Sure beats running around Duluth area by yourself.

Writing in school also includes many examples of level 2 writing: exams, homework, informal reports, group reports, and second or third drafts. We use level 2 writings to explain, summarize, inform, or further develop a discovery activity. Readers need to understand the writing easily without unusual or unknown writing conventions hampering communication. Because level 2 is more formal than level 1, an added degree of correctness in spelling, punctuation, and grammar is appropriate. However, the writing does not need to appear flawless. If a teacher insists that every word must be spelled correctly, then students may use easy-to-spell words rather than words that reflect the nuances or connotations that make the writing lively and interesting. The same is true for sentence variety. If a teacher stresses correct punctuation, the majority of sentences will be simple ones because of uncertainties about comma and semicolon use. Although students may have the opportunity to look over a piece of writing before turning it in, they usually do not have the time or resources many need to make corrections. It is enough that, depending on the age and ability of the students, the writing reflects well-known conventions of writing skills, without undue emphasis on form over content. Figure 3–2 is an example of a level 2 assignment from a middle school. The teacher, Sara Argabright, using an idea from her science textbook (Prentice-Hall, 1986), had students creatively name a micro-organism, write a description of it, and draw an illustration.

Figure 3–3, also at level 2, is an assignment for older students. The activity designed by the teacher, Bill Olien, was based on a field trip to a fruit home landscape. Level 2 is appropriate because his purpose was to help students notice more on the field trip, record observations, and reflect on what they learned. Carrying the assignment to level 3 would not benefit the activity.

Level 3

The most formal of the levels is appropriate only for special projects. The audience is outside our immediate circle of acquaintances, family, and co-workers and may include readers we do not know. The writing alone projects an image of who we are and what we know. We are not present to explain what we meant to say

FIGURE 3-2   Level 2 Writing

Brandy Ferrell

Eugene Euglena (flagellate) Eugene is a champion horse rider with his whip-like flagellum. He had a record time of 48 sec. on the track. When asked what he was going to have for dinner, he said that he was going home for a nice home made meal. And for all those ladies, he's single and plans to remane that way. (He's a loner)

Eugene Euglena

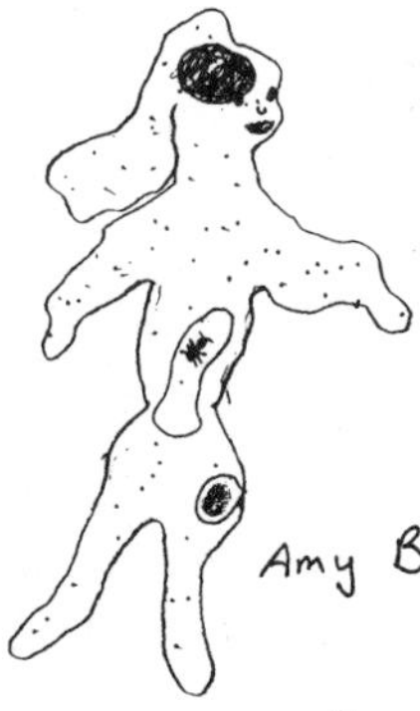

Amy Ba

Mira Domsky

I think that Amy Ba should be in the Hall of Fame because she managed to streach herself until she was one foot long! Ever since the bionary fission that gave her life she has wanted to win the "Streach Your Pseudopods" contest. Now she has finally made her dream come true and is going to settle down for fission to enlarge the Amoeba family. Her picture is on the other side of this paper.

FIGURE 3-3(a)   A Level 2 Assignment for Older Students

Fruit in the Home Landscape
SUMMARY RESPONSE REPORT
(due Wednesday, November 23)

Your Name: *Jon Mason*

Site 1: Spurlock Residence

A. Ideas from this site that I liked and would be useful in our Fruit Teaching Garden are:

- like mixing of plant w/ fruits
- like the sheltered area.
- like natural posts
- idwlling

B. My suggestions of alternatives to consider for this site are:

- use a single wire trellis
- using a net so birds won't eat seeds
- pruning & training (proper)
- create more w/ flow

or that the spelling error is really just a typo. Résumés, job applications, business letters, stories, poems, reports, and essays are all examples of level 3.

The speech scale comparable to level 3 writing is used for formal occasions, perhaps a formal speech given to a wide audience such as a graduation speech. The audience may be a single person, but someone we want to impress with our knowledge and style. Most likely, in these situations, we are judged by the way we present ourselves through speaking.

Level 3 writing is formal and, therefore, always a polished draft that has gone through all of the stages of the writing process: discovery activities, multiple revisions, editing, and proofreading.

Though appropriate for some school writing, it is not the mainstay of the writing activities and assignments we use in the classroom. Teachers should assign level 3 sparingly, and only for major projects or those that include readers outside the classroom. To use level three for all school writing is like Joos's example of

---

FIGURE 3-3(b)   A Level 2 Assignment for Older Students (continued)

by Jon Mason   I really enjoyed this field trip. I wish we could have done this sort of thing before during lab. The first palce we visited was the Spurlock residence. Several of the ideas that I liked from his garden were his mixing of ornamental plants with fruit plants. This idea is very important for our garden project. The sheltered area with all the trees around it where this garden was located was also very nice for wind protection and providing a microclimate. However, this was also a hazard in that there was not enough air flow. I also liked his natural posts for his trellises, this added a look of naturalness. The other item that I was impressed with was the labeling on all the plants. This is very important for us to remember for our project. The only suggestions I had other than the ones already mentioned are using a net so that birds and other animals cannot eat the fruit, and hiring people to prune all his plants correctly.

The next place we visited was the Yenke residence. The items that I really liked were the sheltered area, the retaining wall, and the spacers and guidewires used on his fruit trees. I think retaining walls in our garden would add a sense of confinement to our project and would be very beneficial. I also think that having spacers and different other training methods would be useful training methods for visiters to our garden. The alternatives I would suggest for this site are to cut the oak tree down that is nearest to the garden area becuase this would provide a lot more sun to flow into this area. I also think the mulch was applied a little too heavy for all the crops. Too much mulch could cause diseases and other problems. The only other item I wrote down was to learn how to prune correctly and to place plants with consideration of how they are going to grow.

Overall, I think this trip was very beneficial for the class because we got to see hands on how the topics we are learning can benefit a homeowner. I also think it was helpfull to try and help these homeowners on the problems they had relating to fruit.

---

setting every clock to Central Standard Time. Purpose and audience must determine the levels.

Because of the variety of writing activities students need to help them learn, a variety of levels should be present in the classroom, also. How frequently each level is used depends on how the writing aids in student learning.

Frequency of Levels

Level 1

The fact that writing is used as a tool for learning necessitates that level 1 is the most common type of writing in school. Level 1 is a daily occurrence when critical thinking plays a dominant role in a classroom. Level 1 writing gives students a means of putting their thoughts on paper without concern over writing conventions. Our minds go so much faster than our ability to write that we need freedom from restrictions to get our thoughts down. Also, level 1 works when students are muddling through, concentrating on a problem. The writing may come slowly, but the intensity of thinking requires that one's self-editor stay out of the way. If we become distracted by a concern over spelling or punctuation, our train of thought is disrupted and we lose focus. Specific examples of level 1 writing are numerous:

- Notes from assigned reading in the textbook
- Lecture notes
- Lists
- Notes from a small-group discussion
- Questions from homework
- Brainstorming the beginning of a longer writing
- Free writing
- Mapping, webbing, first attempts at organizing
- Developing questions for use in writing reports
- All journal writing
- All first drafts

Because much level 1 writing is for organizing thoughts, helping with memory, figuring things out, and keeping track of information, it is important that students have frequent opportunities to do this level of writing.

Level 2

Next in frequency of use is level 2 writing, which usually is read and often evaluated by a teacher. Classmates may read the writing without the presence of the author, so the work must stand on its own. Punctuation and other writing conventions now become important for helping readers understand the writer's intended meaning. Level 2 writing may occur a few times a week; once a week is not uncommon. If teachers are assigning level 2 writing every day, they should switch to more level 1 assignments because most writing should not be read or evaluated by a teacher. When level 2 is used more frequently than level 1, students are writing to inform a teacher about what they know more than to use writing as part of a thinking process. Level 2 is for answering questions in a more organized, planned way in order to share writing with a wider audience, whether that audience be the teacher or classmates, and to exhibit what the writer knows. Although these are important reasons for writing, the purposes for level 1 are essential to develop thoughtful, clear writing in the student's own voice, important for all the levels of writing.

Examples of level 2 writing include the following:

- Exams
- Drafts
- Homework assignments
- Summaries
- Reaction papers
- Responses

In the writing process, the drafting stage may begin with level 1, but drafting is mainly at level 2 as students write to an audience beyond themselves.

Level 3

Because of the time involved in producing a level 3 piece of writing and the few times writing is intended for a wide audience, this level must be reserved for only occasional use. If students have the opportunity to work on a level 3 project every four to six weeks, this is sufficient time for them to learn how to prepare an error-free paper, using the final steps in the writing process. If level 3 papers are assigned more often, the amount of writing in the class drops considerably. There simply is not enough time in the day, week, or year for students to work on level 3 frequently and still have opportunities for other activities. What gets pushed aside are all the discovery techniques, variety of activities, creative opportunities, critical thinking. What remains is an outdated style of writing where every piece needs to look as if it were written for publication. Although publishing is important, it is unrealistic and unfair to expect students to limit all of their writing to this mode. Teachers do not; no one does in the real world. Misguided thinking still encourages some teachers to believe this is the only type of writing appropriate for school. The students are the losers in this artificial situation, where fluency is sacrificed for "correctness."

However, teaching the value of an error-free piece and the knowledge needed to produce one is also important. At times, it is essential that we pay as much attention to form as to content, although it is never appropriate to pay *more* attention to form than to content. That would be something like decorating a cardboard cake with beautiful designs—beautiful to look at, but lacking interesting or even palatable texture and substance. Students are more apt to understand the value of polished writing and to do their best work if the reason for the careful editing is realistic—a job application, letter to the editor, or submission for publication. But publication does not have to go beyond the school to require students' best work in creating the error-free copy. At times, level 3 is appropriate even if the work is intended only for the teacher and parent(s). For example, a culminating activity at the conclusion of a unit might be a carefully thought-out report or project that represents a great deal of work on the part of the student. Even though the writing does not go beyond the classroom and is not published for a wider audience, the amount of effort put into the work calls for a polished final copy and is the ideal place to teach and emphasize final editing and proofreading skills. Examples of level 3 writings then could include the following:

- Business letters
- Job applications
- Writing for newspapers
- Submissions to a school anthology
- Essays for contests
- Final reports and projects

Figure 3–4 summarizes the three levels of writing.

FIGURE 3-4   Levels of Writing

Level 1

Style: Informal—in speech, similar to talking to close friends
Audience: Writer and, in some cases, teacher and peer group
Function: Thinking through writing, organizing thoughts, generating ideas, developing fluency, helping with memory
Form: Note-taking, journal writing, responses, lists, brainstorming, mapping, first drafts.
Evaluation: Content only, often not evaluated at all; mechanics, word usage, organization, spelling, and grammar are not considered.

Level 2

Style: More formal—in speech, similar to talking to an audience outside one's close circle of friends
Audience: Writer, classmates, teacher, parents; audience may not be known well.
Function: Organizing thoughts coherently, developing ideas, explaining, informing; practical—to get work done
Form: Exams, homework, multiple drafts, reports, summaries
Evaluation: Evaluated for content and form; common writing conventions expected as appropriate for grade and ability level.

Level 3

Style: Formal—in speech, similar to talking to people not known, like giving a formal speech
Audience: Writer, classmates, teacher, parents, audience outside the classroom, an unknown audience
Function: Learning the value of producing error-free writing, reach a wider audience, learning how to edit and proofread
Form: Letters, reports, poetry, research papers, books, final drafts
Evaluation: Content and form of equal weight; all of the writing skills are expected to be correct; neatness and good handwriting or error-free typing important.

Expectations and Evaluations

Whenever any writing is assigned, the teacher and students *must* know the level described in terms of audience and purpose. In most cases the teacher decides on the appropriate level. Once students become familiar with the use of levels, however, they, too, may choose the appropriate level, as long as their reasons are not in conflict with the obvious purpose. It is the purpose of the assignment that determines the level. When a teacher is not clear about what he or she wants a particular assignment to accomplish, neither are the students, and much confusion results over the expectations of the teacher:

- How many details should the writer include?
- What about organization?
- How about punctuation, spelling, and grammar?
- How should the writing look?

By determining the level before telling students about the assignment, the teacher knows how he or she will evaluate it. That information should be shared with the writers. When students know the level, they do not ask if spelling counts. They know it does not in level 1, that it does for familiar words in level 2, and that it does for every word in level 3. The same guidelines apply to every writing convention. For example, organization may or may not exist at level 1, depending on the particular writing task, but the writer knows that the presence or lack of organization is not part of the evaluation. In level 2, organization is necessary in order for readers to gain understanding, although some organization may be added as an afterthought and shown with arrows, insertions, and paragraph markers. This is especially appropriate on an exam, where the teacher's purpose for the writing is to check students' knowledge about a subject, not to see if they can write in an organized fashion when time is limited and stress is likely high.

An argument that some people put forth who believe that all writing should be level 3 is that students must learn how to write more formal papers. Yes, they should, but in assigning a level 3 piece approximately every four weeks and helping students learn how to revise, edit, and proofread it, the teacher provides enough instruction and practice for students. To do more than this takes away valuable time from other types of writing and activities.

Length of Written Work by Levels

Because audience and purpose determine levels, length has no relation to the level of writing. Level 1 writings often are the longest, as in journal writing or extensive notes. A one-page letter for publication is a level 3. The issue of length is important to bring up with students so that they learn to keep audience and purpose foremost in their minds when deciding on the degree of formality of a piece of writing. The fact that something is short does not mean it can be tossed off with little thought. A poem, letter, or explanation written for publication may take weeks of revising before the author decides he or she is finished.

As much as possible, students should have a say in establishing purpose, although a teacher must help guide students to realize what purpose is for. Younger students, when asked why they are writing something, often answer, "Because the teacher told me to." In a broad sense this is true, but teachers have a purpose in making the assignment and need to relay this to the class so that students always know why they are doing the assignment. How the assignment is carried out, including length, remains the responsibility of the student.

Writing Levels within Assignments

Many assignments use more than one level of writing. Level 3 always includes levels 1 and 2 because any published writing must go through the entire writing process. The beginning stages of the writing process are level 1 while the drafting is level 2. As examples, three unit projects are described next.

Science

The unit is "Adaptation for Survival." Specifically, students are looking at how animals adapt to changing environments. As the unit progresses, students keep notes on readings, films, and lectures (level 1). Every few days, they read over their own notes looking for connections and patterns. They jot down questions that come up about areas that are confusing or areas of particular interest. Students meet in groups to compare their notes and then write a report based on their material to hand in (level 2). The unit project is to choose one animal and research its adaptation necessary for survival. As students read additional material for the individual project, they keep notes (level 1), and then write a first draft (level 1). They meet in response groups, revise (level 2), and gradually the writing takes shape as they continue to revise (level 2). Students meet with a writing partner for editing and proofreading and then write a final copy (level 3).

English

Students read *To Kill a Mockingbird* by Harper Lee. As they read, they keep a response journal, writing their thoughts about the characters; their reactions to the story; and related thoughts from their own lives, other fiction, or real-life stories (level 1). Students meet in groups to share their responses and thoughts about the novel. Individually, students write a character sketch of Dill or Boo. The sketch is handed in and evaluated by the teacher (level 2). As students continue reading and responding in their journals, the teacher reads their journals and writes comments (level 1). Near the end of the book, students write a short paper on how Scout changes throughout the book. They first write a rough draft and read it in response groups (level 1). Students revise the draft and turn it in for evaluation (level 2). Students view the movie based on the novel, write responses (level 1), and discuss in groups. As a group, they write a short paper comparing the effectiveness of the book versus the film (level 2). There is no level 3 for this assignment.

If students are not working on a final project, levels 1 and 2 are all that are necessary to engage them as active learners. Perhaps eventually students will write a level 3 paper comparing this novel to others they read, but level 3 writing is not required to make sure students read and understand.

English as a Second Language

ESL teacher Gail Servoss describes related activities that include all three levels she uses to help her students become fluent in English.

Level 1
Students are given a picture showing a situation and more than one character. They write a dialogue from one character's viewpoint. Students read the dialogues aloud, and the others guess whom the student is writing about.

Level 2
Each student receives a picture and writes a scenario or description of it in a limited time period. Students then get into groups of three to five and read their stories to each other. The others interrupt the writer with questions concerning details. Each writer must answer the question in writing.

Level 3
Students choose a picture from a magazine and write a story from it. Vocabulary is brainstormed individually with the teacher or with peers. The writing process is followed, and the stories are published in a class book.

In later chapters, more detailed assignments further illustrate the use of the levels in content area writing.

Summary

Standards vary in many areas of our life, and we adjust our behavior accordingly. Writing, too, has different standards and should reflect these differences. The writing standards are categorized into three levels, comparable to different levels of speech. The relationship between purpose and audience determines the level of writing. Once the level is established, the type and degree of evaluation are clear to both students and teachers. Level 1 is used the most frequently, usually daily; level 2 is assigned once or twice a week; level 3 occurs only once every three to five weeks. The length of the students' writing has no relationship to the level. Several levels are used throughout assignments.

Discussion Questions

1. What connections exist between real-life writing and school writing?
2. In what situations are people told they are speaking incorrectly?
3. When is it appropriate to correct someone's speech? When is it appropriate to correct someone's writing?
4. How does the use of writing levels compare to your experiences of writing in school?
5. How do we determine what standard of writing conventions to use for the different kinds of writing we do?

Suggested Activities

1. List 8 to 10 writing activities or assignments you could use in your discipline to help students learn.
2. Explain the purpose for each of these activities.
3. Assign a level to each one based on the purpose. Discuss your list with other students who will teach similar subjects.
4. Keep a list of *all* the writing you do for one week. At the end of the week, assign levels to each one. What were the purposes of the writings?
5. Design a writing assignment for your discipline that incorporates all three levels. Include several level 1 activities, two or three level 2 activities, and one level 3 activity.

References

Hymes, Dell. "Models of the Interaction of Language and Social Life." In John J. Gumperz & Dell Hymes, eds., *Directions in Sociolinguistics* (pp. 35–71). New York: Holt, Rinehart & Winston, 1972.

Joos, Martin. *The Five Clocks.* New York: Harcourt, Brace & World, 1961.

Lehning, James R. "Writing about History and Writing in History." *The History Teacher,* 26,(3), May 1993.

Martin, Nancy, Peter Medway, Harold Smith, &

Pat D'Arcy. "Why Write?" In Nancy Martin, Peter Medway, & Harold Smith, eds., *Writing Across the Curriculum* (pp. 34–59). Montclair, NJ: Boynton/Cook, 1984.

Miller Jr., James E., & Stephen N. Judy. *Writing in Reality.* New York: Harper & Row, 1978.

Rubin, Donald L. Introduction. In Susan Hynds & Donald L. Rubin, eds., *Perspectives on Talk and Learning* (pp. 1–17). Urbana, IL: National Council of Teachers of English, 1990.

4

JOURNALS

There are, though, a number of tricks you can teach yourself in order to free the writing self, and the essence of these is to give yourself permission to fail. The best place for permission is a private place, and for that reason a writer's journal is an essential, likely to be the source of originality, ideas, experimentation, and growth. Keep a journal.—JANET BURROWAY, 1992, p. 3

Prereading Questions

1. How might personal writing and school writing be related?
2. If you ever kept a diary or journal, what was the purpose, and was it a successful project?
3. Why are historical journals of such high interest to the public?
4. What kinds of writing might go into a journal?
5. What purposes could journal writing fulfill in school?

Introduction

Journals are an important part of writing across the curriculum. Originally, journals were used only as a way of helping students become fluent writers by providing a place where they could write anything they wanted without fear of receiving negative evaluations from a teacher. Personal journals, as these are called, allow writers to express thoughts freely so that writing becomes a natural extension of thinking, feeling, reacting, and remembering. Writing about an experience gives the writer opportunities to reflect and make sense of that experience. Although there still is an important place in the curriculum for unstructured and undirected journal writing, the uses have expanded beyond this general purpose, particularly in writing throughout the curriculum.

Purposes of Journals

Toby Fulwiler, who has extensively developed the use of journals across the curriculum, uses journals in class for discussion, for small-group activity, to clarify hazy issues, to reinforce learning experience, and to stimulate students' imaginations. "The journal can become the first articulation for any idea or experiment" (Fulwiler, 1980, p. 15). Also, they can become a source of thoughtful reflection on what one has read, heard, thought, or learned.

Journals vary depending on the subject, teacher, and purpose, but all have some features in common. Fulwiler describes the formal features as follows:

> frequent entries—writing often to catch one's thoughts
> long entries—to develop a thought or find a new one
> self-sponsored entries—without teacher prompts
> chronology of entries—systematic documentation. (Fulwiler, 1987, p. 3)

Fulwiler suggests that students use a looseleaf notebook for their journal. They should divide it into sections, one for each class and one for private entries (1987, p. 7). Even if the journal is used for only one class, the looseleaf format is handy because students can continue to write when they have handed in a section for the teacher to read.

Journals provide a place for students to think through what they are studying, to record what they already know before starting a topic, to keep track of what they learn, and in general to help themselves learn content. Specific ways to enlist the help of journal writing in the teaching and learning of subject matter are the focus of this chapter.

Personal Journals

Students write in their journals in a variety of ways. Those who like to draw often fill pages with sketches. Other students might include cartoons and stories clipped from the newspaper. At one time, I required that students write their thoughts and feelings, not just what they did during the day. Later, however, I realized I was putting unfair restrictions on their personal writing. For some students, recording what happens throughout the day is meaningful and important to them, and it is inappropriate for teachers to tell them it isn't what they should write.

Two experiences made this apparent to me. The first is from a middle school class where a boy always wrote a simple factual account—when he got up, what he had for breakfast, and so on—but never expressed any reaction to the list of events. Despite my urging, his journal remained the same throughout the year. A few years later, he stopped by my classroom and, in the course of the visit, thanked me for getting him started on journal writing. He had continued to keep a journal and found it helpful and enjoyable. I knew then that a teacher cannot decide for another person what he or she should write in a personal journal.

The second experience comes from the writing project I direct. One of the participants brought in a diary her great-grandmother had kept diligently for a number of years. The brief entries recorded the weather and a line or two about ordinary events, but nothing about the richness of her life. Yet, when I read the journals, a sense of her personality came through and an image of her as an individual developed. Sometimes ordinary things tell a great deal about one's life and should not be discarded as uninteresting or unimportant.

If students have no experience in writing, the personal journal is a good place to begin developing fluency. When students are first given an opportunity to write whatever they want, many do not know what to write. School writing is often prescriptive, leaving little freedom for writers to choose their own topics or express their own thoughts. Writing one's own opinions and feelings is foreign to the notion of writing as a school assignment. When the structure of teacher-provided instructions is removed, students often feel at a loss as to where to begin.

Teachers can help by offering writing suggestions to students. However, the ideas are just that—suggestions—and if students have their own ideas, so much the better. Several kinds of questions can spark writing ideas for the students who have trouble getting started.

- Open-ended:
  — The reasons I like my favorite television show are . . .
  — The places I'd most like to travel are . . . .
  — I'm most at peace when . . .
  — My favorite place to be is . . .
  — If I could be any character from a TV show or a book, I would be _____ because . . .
  — My favorite TV commercial is . . .
  — If I could make a TV commercial, it would be about . . .
  — My favorite joke is . . .
  — What I remember best from last year is . . .
  — What I like least about school is . . .
- Making lists:
  — My 10 favorite (or most disliked) songs are . . .
  — The 5 things I would most like to change about this school are . . .
  — Name your 3 favorite people and describe them.
  — Name 3 people you admire the most and tell why.
  — List the qualities of a good teacher (or a good friend).
  — List 10 things you do every day. Choose one that is a favorite and tell why.
  — Name 10 things that could never happen in your life. Choose the one you most wish would happen.

- Descriptive ideas:
  — Describe how to keep score in a sport you play.
  — Describe your favorite kind of animal.
  — Tell about a funny incident that happened to you or to someone in your family.
  — If you could change anything about your life, what would it be?
  — What would you most like to be famous for?
  — If you could change places with one of your parents for a day, what would you do?
- Responding:
  — The teacher writes a quote on the board every day, and the student may write a response to it.
  — The teacher writes a coded message each day, and students try to decipher it.
  — Students generate a topic or question of the day.
- Imagination starters:
  — You are in Antarctica exploring uncharted areas when you come upon . . .
  — You are deep-sea diving and discover . . .
  — An unknown relative dies leaving you a fortune, but to claim it you must . . .

Evaluating Personal Journals

Journals, though often read by a teacher, are never evaluated in any way: not by length, spelling, punctuation, handwriting, or completeness of sentences. The goal of developing fluency is not attainable if the writing is judged and evaluated. The purpose of this type of journal is to provide a place for students to write on a regular basis, free from concern about punctuation, grammar, spelling, or handwriting. At first, students may find the freedom from writing conventions difficult to believe, especially if they have had their writing overly criticized for lack of standard usage and punctuation. It seems too good to be true that they can write and not have to worry about commas and spelling. Janet Burroway in *Writing Fiction* describes a journal as "an intimate, a friend that will accept you as you are" (Burroway, 1992, p. 3). Unless we keep our internal editor silenced, worrying about correct conventions interrupts our flow of thought. Another way of describing journal writing is to say it is at level 1. Then, how a teacher evaluates journal writing is clear to students and teacher alike.

Although journals are not evaluated, they are *read* by the teacher. Although it takes time, reading journals is important for building rapport between student and teacher. It provides opportunities for dialogue, something often hard to accomplish in the classroom. Teachers read what each student has written and respond in writing. As a rule, it is not necessary to write in-depth comments. Students mostly want an interested listener, not an advice-giver, unless they specifically ask for advice. Writing responses back and forth helps establish a feeling of trust and respect between student and teacher as they get to know each other better. When teachers take the time to write, it builds self-esteem in students because they know what they write in the journals is taken seriously.

Extended Use of Personal Journals

Occasionally, a topic comes up that interests or affects all the students: a national election, a local news or human interest story, a disaster, or a joyful or sad event in the life of someone the students know. At such times, writing in their journals helps students to think through their emotions. Journal entries might provide a basis for classroom discussion. When students write first, and then use their writing for a starting point in class discussion, they find it easier to talk, and more students will join in.

Personal writing also can provide a starting point for a story or essay. Fiction writing is often based on one's own experiences, and examples for essays come from real-life events. Knowing that their personal journals, as well as those connected to assignments, are valid in the class helps students know that they are important as individuals who have much to offer. Students' own experiences play an important part in a class, and the personal journal gives them the means for sharing if teachers periodically provide time for students to discuss in small groups what they have written.

Frequency for Using Personal Journals

Personal journals do not have to continue for the entire nine months of the school year. Student (and teacher) interest is higher if journals are required only for intermittent periods. When teachers assign journals, however, it is important that students write in them on a regular basis. It doesn't matter how much they write, or what they write, but it does matter that they make a steady habit of writing (Burroway, 1992, p. 4). To help ease the teacher's job, each class can use personal journals during a different time period. Because this type of journal is not tied to class assignments or topics, one class can begin the first week of school, another four weeks later, and so on. Also, teachers can stagger the dates the journals are handed in so they have a manageable number to read at one time.

Learning Logs

Using a journal as a place to facilitate learning is indispensable for writing across the curriculum. Unlike personal journals, learning logs are directly related to specific class activity. Writing in a learning log is usually a discovery activity leading to a better understanding of a topic, concept, or unit. Although the writing is a discovery activity, that does not mean it occurs only at the beginning of an assignment. All through a unit, students use the log as a place to clarify their understanding of what they know and what they need to know.

At the beginning of a unit or lesson, both teachers and students find it helpful if students define or explain what they are going to study. For teachers, this is a way of finding out what their students know about a topic. When we use a word that is familiar to us, we cannot take for granted that students have the necessary background information to understand. For example, we cannot assume students know what *geology* means, although when we tell them the next unit is one on geology, no one is apt to ask what the word means. A good place to start is to have students write in their learning logs a definition of geology—or the solar system, or Greece—whatever the topic is. They might share their definitions in groups and come up with a definition they all agree on. There is no right or wrong response; the purpose is to discover where the teacher needs to begin the topic.

For some topics, rather than define a word, students begin by writing everything they know about the topic. The entry serves as a pretest, not for a teacher's evaluation, but for the students to look at near the end of a unit to see how much they have learned. This is especially helpful for topics where misinformation can be a serious problem—for example, in learning about Native Americans, the Hmong, or any other minority group. Without the learning log entry, biases may never surface and, therefore, may not be dealt with.

Writing is not the only way prior knowledge is expressed. Drawing often explains more than words, especially in areas where thoughts are more subconscious than clearly defined. The solar system is a good example of a topic where drawing may tell more than words. Asking students to draw what comes to mind when they think of a particular culture or country also may reveal more than words. Using this type of activity before beginning an area of study helps teachers realize where to begin, what areas to fill in, and what prejudices and incorrect assumptions to address.

Not all learning log writing is read by a teacher; most of the writing is only for the students themselves. Before beginning a unit, students can write a list of questions they want to answer during the course of the study. These questions help to focus their reading. Or the learning log can become a place to summarize what they have read or what they remember from a lecture. Also, students can record questions and problems that come up when they are doing their homework—for example, math that was confusing. In the next math class, they know exactly what to ask the teacher. Focused questions are a great help in learning because they are relevant to the individual student.

Learning log writing is appropriate for a wide variety of subjects. The following list provides a few examples across the curriculum:

- Draw and/or write everything you know about Berlin.
- List as many habitats as you can. The list may serve as informational or fictional writing.
- Describe how the earth moves.
- List five questions that pique your curiosity about Ancient Greece.
- What would you do if left alone in a desert?
- List the advantages and disadvantages of living in [the name of your town].
- List the pro and cons of burning forest areas.
- Write the pro and cons of busing students.
- Describe hail and explain what causes it.

- Define *osmosis.*
- Describe a virus.
- Define *hypothesis.*

Learning logs are useful as a safe place for students to write descriptions, definitions, and predictions. Often, learning logs are the first step to learning about a subject. Students can try out their ideas and thoughts without fear of reprisal. Prior knowledge is an important part of learning, and the logs are the place to record what students think they know about something. Also, students can use the logs for responding to homework and for informal self-evaluation.

Having students record what they have accomplished in a class is an excellent way for a teacher to check student understandings. The following example was written by Amanda Viaca, a twelfth-grade student:

Journal 12/5/94

Lately we've been working on databases and we have covered many different functions of the database. We've already learned about what a database is made up of, (records, fields, etc.) how to create one, what matches, finds, and filters are and how to create and use them, and this last week we learned how to do a sort on the database and create and edit reports.

Sorts are handy because they let you find records better and display information more clearly because it is in a certain order. You can create them by going to the Data menu and going Sort . . . and then using the pop up menu for fields to choose a field to sort by and then you can choose descending (Z–A OR 9–0) or ascending orders (A–Z OR 0–9). You can also do multiple sorts which means that within one sort, you can organize that part of the sort with another sort. But there is one thing to remember when doing multiple sorts, do the secondary (least important) first and then in order to the primary sort going last. Another handy thing about sorts is that you can save them as a different file name (in fact, you have to or else you will save over the original or natural order of your database) and use them at a later date without having to resort. Sorts are also handy because you can put a database in a certain order, save it, and then create a report to reflect that information and then print it out. This is good because it lets you create reports with the same database but in different orders that suit your needs.

Reports are created by selecting records you want and in what order in the report by highlighting them or by using a sort or filter. Then you go to the Report menu and choose new report. Then you name the report and click the create button. You can format the report you created by: selecting fields that you want to print while leaving out the rest, by doing a subtotal or total (by selecting the field you want to total or subtotal and then choosing the Sum. This Field tool or Subtotal when contents change), by turning off the grid (Form menu—choose Show Grid to turn on and off), by changing page size and margins through page setup and options, and orientations through page setup and orientation choices, or by changing the appearance of fields (or the whole report) and changing the font, size, or style. Rearranging fields is also an option. To do this you simply grab hold of the field name while in report view and drag it to where you want it. The field will be placed to the left of the highlighted field or you can choose not to show it in the report by dragging it to the right of the right margin marker.

This whole database business has a bunch more to do than I thought it would. I'm glad we're almost done. (We *are* almost done aren't we?)

Project Journals

Project journals are intended for long-term projects like a science investigation, environmental study, cultural history, or other integrated assignments. This type of journal follows the progress of a student's work from the beginning of the assignment to the end. Using a project journal helps students remember deadlines, organize tasks, and keep track of where they are. The journal is handed in along with the final project.

The first entry in the journal is to write the assignment when the teacher explains it to the class. Students then meet in groups and discuss their understanding of the requirements of the assignment. Although teachers always ask if there are any questions about the assignment, many students may not ask questions, although they do not understand or are confused about some points. Students may not wish to ask questions in a whole-class group out of embarrassment or a reluctance to speak up in large groups, but in small groups they will express frustration about not understanding what they are supposed to do. After they meet in groups, they write the assignment again in their journal and jot down any further questions they have about the explanation and the teacher's expectations. They may show it to the teacher to make sure they are on the right track. Halfway through a project is not a good time to discover that they misunderstood the nature of the assignment. If they do not write the explanation and the related questions, students often will state in class that they don't know what they should do or "what the teacher wants"; this puts the onus of the responsibility on the teacher. A recurring theme throughout this book is that students must accept responsibility for their own learning. Writing an assignment in their own words to be sure they understand is part of that responsibility.

After the assignment is clearly understood, a teacher often has students begin the project by writing what they already know about the topic. As students begin to collect information from their reading, from listening to lectures, and from other sources such as interviews or films, they record notes in the project journal. Having a single place to record deadlines, requirements, notes, summaries, and questions helps students keep track of their material, no easy task for some, especially at the middle school level. The project journal, a record of the effort and thought that went into the report, becomes part of the final evaluation. It provides a much fairer way to judge their work than having only the final paper determine what they have learned.

Response Journals

Response journals are a place for students to respond to material they read. These journals are an essential part of English and social studies classes, where students use reader response as a critical approach to literature. Reader response theory relies on meaning coming from the relationship of text and reader. Readers respond in writing after a careful reading of the literature and develop understandings from their own and others' responses.

Over fifty years ago, Louise Rosenblatt began her work on a transactional approach to literature based on her research. She defined the *transaction* as an interaction between reader and text that creates meaning. The reader "brings to the work personality traits, memories of past events, present needs and preoccupations, a particular mood of the moment" (Rosenblatt, 1976, pp. 30–31). Students are specific human beings with individual hearts and minds, and they bring different experiences to the act of reading. The teacher's job is to help create a relationship between the individual piece of literature and the individual student (Rosenblatt, 1976, p. 33), and the response journal is a means by which this happens.

A major difficulty in encouraging students to relate to literature through writing in a journal is the notion that understanding literature means knowing an underlying meaning to which only certain people have access, for instance the teacher and maybe the author. "The meaning" in this sense does not exist. Rosenblatt stresses that meaning comes from a reader's response to the literature; because each reader is unique, everyone does not arrive at "one true meaning" as defined by someone else. When teachers explain to students what a piece of literature means, a dichotomy is set up with the teacher as the holder of the truth and the students, as those who are uninformed. Such an arrangement promotes passivity in students, who wait to be told what to believe rather than discovering meaning on their own.

Robert E. Probst, an educator whose work focuses on implementing response theory in the classroom, explains that readers must feel free to deal first with their own reactions to a text, and then, later, to revise and expand their notions (Probst, 1988, p. 31). Students share their responses in small groups and gain an understanding from others' responses of the different ways of looking at a text. Probst points out that students must feel comfortable with each other for response journals to succeed (p. 33).

When keeping a response journal, students write what the story makes them think about and relate their own feelings and experiences to the reading. They can respond to an entire passage, a word, a phrase, or a general feeling evoked by the reading. Students who are not accustomed to responding to literature may need some guidance at first. A teacher may pose questions that provide some structure:

- In what ways do the characters remind you of someone you know?
- What happens in the story that makes you think of experiences you have had?
- Describe the connections between the story and others you have read, or television shows or movies.
- If you were one of the characters, how would you act or what would you change?

When writing questions for students, it is important for teachers to avoid those with yes-or-no answers. We want students to engage with the text, to think about their reactions, and a simple yes or no does not require much thought.

As students become comfortable with response journals, the questions are not necessary or even desirable. We want students to have freedom to follow their own thoughts and feelings, not ones prescribed by a teacher. However, students are required to think about what they read; a simplistic "I don't like this story" or "It's boring" is not acceptable. Students must explain *why* they think so. What did they dislike about the story? What parts are boring? Why? The teacher can go over the reading with them and ask questions: "What part didn't you care for?" "What do you think of this?" "What did you think when the character did this?" Shallow answers or nonresponses often come from a sense of inadequacy on the part of a student. Perhaps students have been told previously that their answers were incorrect, and they are unwilling to take a chance, or their self-esteem in general may be low. Teachers need patience and understanding to rebuild trust so that students are willing to take a chance by expressing an opinion.

Writer's Notebook

A writer's notebook is a tool for responding to the world around us. As the name implies, the notebook is the basis for writing. It is not used for a particular assignment but is ongoing, a source of ideas, images, characters, and stories. Keeping a writer's notebook makes us more aware of our surroundings. Joan Didion, in an essay titled "On Keeping a Notebook," explains that for her the purpose of the journal is not to have "an accurate factual record of what I have been doing or thinking" (1968, p. 133). Her recordings are more about "how it felt to me" (p. 134). Although many people believe that only writers of fiction find a writer's notebook helpful, that is not the case. Learning to record what you see and hear "will enrich your perceptions of, and reactions to, many aspects of your life, for the creative attitude affects all you do and see" (Rico, 1983, p. 21). We all benefit from noticing the world around us, from opening our eyes to the inconsistencies, the surprises, the wonder of life.

Because the notebook is a response to our immediate surroundings, it needs to be small enough to carry around all the time. Bits of overheard conversation, signs, names of people or places, a person's action that catches our attention—all are jotted down in the writer's notebook. The entries may or may not ever make their way into one's writing, but they do awaken an awareness of language and images that are too soon forgotten unless we record them.

Becky Olien, a teacher and writer of both fiction and nonfiction, divides her notebook into sections so that locating specific entries is easier. She uses the following categories:

1. Situations
2. Descriptions of people
3. Descriptions of places and things
4. Words and phrases
5. Resources, words of advice, books

Olien's categories work for her because they fit her purpose of using what she sees and hears as possible material for her writing. For writers who keep notebooks for different reasons, a different system may work better—or no system at all. What is important is that the notebook is used consistently. "It doesn't matter what you write and it doesn't matter very much how much, but it does matter that you make a steady habit of writing" (Burroway, 1992, p. 4).

Class Logs

Class logs have a different purpose from the other journals. The audience for these logs is the class. Their purpose is to keep a record of what goes on in class, and the log is written by a different class member every day. Julie Bronson, a high school teacher, finds class logs indispensable as an organizational tool that benefits teacher and student alike. No longer do students who have been absent come up to her with the question, "Did we do anything in here yesterday?" Bronson does not have to search her memory trying to recall exactly what happened yesterday in a particular class (1989, p. 17). Students find out for themselves by referring to the class log.

A teacher organizes the class log by setting up a schedule at the beginning of the semester. Bronson suggests a written chart with the names of the student writers assigned to each day, so that students, not the teacher, are responsible for remembering (1989, p. 17). Each student begins the log with the date and the names of absent students. Then the student records what goes on in class, notes dates and explanations of assignments, and attaches copies of the day's handouts. Each entry is signed by the writer.

The students are encouraged not only to record what happens in class, but also to comment on the activities. The entries become creative and personal, supporting the active role we want students to assume in the class.

In Bronson's class, the logs go into a pocket folder that is displayed on the chalk rail or a front table. Another teacher, Laura Apfelbeck, sets aside an area on the bulletin board for each class. The day's entry goes on top of the others pinned there. When the stack gets too thick to be secure, she removes some of the older entries and places them in a folder. In whatever ways the entries are displayed, they are kept for an entire year to provide a record that students will enjoy reading and that teachers will find helpful for future planning.

Summary

Journals serve many purposes in the classroom. Response journals encourage students to express themselves and develop the habit of writing. Learning logs are indispensable as part of the learning process and help students clarify their thinking and understand knowledge. Project journals help students organize their time and keep track of their own progress. By recording their reactions and thoughts while reading in response journals, students connect the text with their own life. A writer's notebook helps us become more aware of the world around us by sharpening our senses and observations. Class logs are a record of classroom activities and benefit both teachers and students. Journals are an important part of the writing process.

Discussion Questions

1. How could you as a teacher encourage reluctant students to write in a learning log?
2. How can journals adapt to different learning styles and different ability levels?
3. What are the pros and cons of using journals in every subject? In groups, describe journal writing for one of the following subjects: art, music, industrial arts, computers, physical education.
4. How would you answer a parent who called to tell you journals are a waste of time?
5. How can a teacher safeguard students' privacy when personal journals are used?

Suggested Activities

1. Keep a writer's notebook for two weeks recording all the "language surprises" you observe. These might come from newspaper headlines or articles, overheard conversations, people's names, signs, notices, television shows, radio, or reading.
2. Select a unit you will be studying in one of your college classes. Write down all you already know and what you expect to learn. What particular questions do you want to find answers for?
3. Choose a unit in your discipline you might teach to future students. Plan the uses of journals throughout the unit and specify the purpose for each use.
4. During and/or after a period of study time for another class, perhaps while working math problems or reading a section of the textbook, write what you had difficulty with and then write two or three questions to which you need to find answers for clarification.
5. Select a topic in your content area and describe several specific journal writing ideas that pertain to teaching and learning the subject material.

References

Aaron, Jeffrey. "Integrating Music with Core Subjects." *Music Educators Journal, 80* (6), May 1994, pp. 33–36.

Bronson, Julie. "Captain's Log-Star Date .084 or What Happened Here Yesterday." *Wisconsin English Journal, 31* (2), 1989, pp. 17–20.

Burroway, Janet. *Writing Fiction*, 3rd ed. New York: HarperCollins, 1992.

Didion, Joan. *Slouching towards Bethlehem*. New York: Dell, 1968.

Fulwiler, Toby. "Journals Across the Disciplines." *English Journal*, December 1980, pp. 14–19.

Fulwiler, Toby, ed. *The Journal Book*. Portsmouth: Boynton/Cook, 1987.

Probst, Robert E. *Response Analysis: Teaching Literature in Junior and Senior High School*. Upper Montclair, NJ: Boynton/Cook, 1988.

Rico, Gabriele Lusser. *Writing the Natural Way*. Boston: J. P. Tarcher, 1983.

Rosenblatt, Louise M. *Literature as Exploration*, 3rd ed. New York: Noble and Noble, 1976.

Zimmerman, Enid. "Assessing Students' Progress and Achievements in Art." *Art Education*, November, 1992, pp. 14–24.

5

WRITING AS A MEANS FOR LEARNING

When talking, reading, and writing are orchestrated in the classroom in such a way that each can make its unique contribution to a single end, we have surely harnessed language to learning as powerfully as possible.—JAMES BRITTON, 1989

Prereading Questions

1. What does *study skills* mean to you?
2. How do you study for exams? How might your studying become more effective?
3. Describe a research paper you wrote in high school. How might the process and result of that paper influence how you teach your future students?
4. How can we help students become independent learners? Why is it important?
5. How can teachers help students who have difficulty learning?

Introduction

Earlier chapters discussed the connections learning logs and journals have with learning. This chapter explores the ways specific writing activities help students retain and understand information, activities that fall under the general rubric of study skills. Anne Ruggles Gere, in the introduction to *Roots in the Sawdust*, writes, "Secondary education should provide students a way of thinking, not a set of facts" (Gere, 1985, p. 3). We want to provide students with strategies to help them understand and remember what they read, knowledge of how to do homework successfully and independently, study for tests, and in general become self-sufficient learners.

Strategies for Learning

As educators search for the best way to help students gain and remember information, numerous studies are conducted to compare one method to another. Alison King, a university teacher who specializes in cognitive strategy instruction, designed a study to compare the strategies of self-questioning, summarizing, and reviewing lecture material. Most students rely only on the last strategy: reviewing notes. King found, however, that the more students interacted with the material, the more they comprehended and remembered (King, 1992, p. 304). They performed better on both immediate and delayed comprehension tests when they used the more active learning strategies of summarizing and self-questioning. In summarizing, the students linked key ideas from lectures in their own words. The self-questioning involved constructing questions based on lecture material in preparation for exams. King found that passively rereading lecture notes was the least effective strategy.

A study on learning vocabulary conducted by Carol Dana and Margaret Rodriquez supports the belief the students need time and a method for learning on their own. "Teaching study procedures that students can use on their own time can improve learning and retention of vocabulary" (Dana & Rodriquez, 1992, p. 84). They found that students needed more time than classroom instruction provided if they were to learn the vocabulary. In other words, we need to teach students how to study on their own if they are to be successful.

Notes serve as a way of checking on understanding of the material. Students may not realize they do not understand, and questions they need to ask may not be obvious at the time of a lecture; later, however, going over the material, a student may realize there are gaps or confusing comments. Also, notes help students make connections from one area to another by having the material in a tangible form. The printed material encourages reflection and questioning. Notes from lectures, reading material, group discussions, and films are all important for learning course material.

Improving Note-Taking Skills

Teachers cannot take for granted that students will learn note taking when they are directed to take notes. Taking notes becomes second nature for college students, but we should remind ourselves that students in secondary school rarely know how to take effective notes. As we know, taking notes plays a vital role in learning and is a skill that can be taught and learned. How to take notes is often taught in middle school; however, if students have not learned the skill by high school, then a teacher must teach it regardless of the grade level.

Beginning at about seventh grade, teachers increasingly rely on lectures to transmit information to students. Many students are poor note-takers because they have not been taught strategies (Rafoth et al., 1993). At the secondary level, much learning depends on understanding and retaining information from lectures. Even successful students often fail to note many important ideas during lectures (Potts, 1993, p. 3). To be successful in school, students must learn strategies to use on their own.

Evidence suggests the value to students of taking their own notes, even if these notes are incomplete, as compared to having teachers provide the notes. Teachers need to provide many opportunities for students to practice the skill of note taking. When first teaching students how to take notes from lectures, it is best if teachers lecture for no more than ten minutes. A teacher explains to students that they need to listen carefully to the information they will hear during the lecture, and that they are required to write down what they believe are important points to remember. However, they do not write notes while the teacher is talking. Rafoth agrees that note-taking should not compete with paying attention to lectures (1993, p. 124).

If there are particular names, formulas, dates, or maps the students might have trouble remembering or spelling, the teacher should write the information on the board or overhead for students to copy into their notes after the lecture. Until students become proficient in note-taking—and that does not happen until later in high school—they need to concentrate on listening to the speaker. If they try to get notes down while listening, they will not hear all of the lecture. Trying to write what was already said *while* listening to what is now being said is extremely difficult.

After the presentation, students, without any discussion, write down the major points. Then they share what they have written in a whole-class discussion. The teacher guides the discussion by asking why a point needs to be recorded or why a student believes it is important. The importance of abbreviating and not writing complete sentences, but getting just enough down on paper so that the reader remembers and understands the information, needs to be stressed. Over a period of several days, the teacher continues the practice by lecturing for short periods and asking students to share in small groups what they have written. Gradually lengthening the lectures until they are twenty to thirty minutes long helps students acquire the skill of note-taking. During the longer lectures, the teacher pauses about every ten minutes to allow students to write down the notes and ask questions.

To help students in note-taking, some teachers provide an outline or format for students to fill out. Bonnie Potts has reviewed several investigations that examined the efficiency of note-taking structures for students. The structures include outlines, matrices, or skeletal forms; the last proved the most beneficial because the main ideas of the lecture provided hierarchical relationships, and spaces were left for students to fill in the detailed information (Potts, 1993, p. 4). Whether forms are provided or not, Potts suggests the following points to consider when lecturing: Speak slowly. Segment the lectures, pausing every six or seven minutes to allow students to write notes. Allow students to devote time to listening and then have them paraphrase the material during the pauses. Teachers can give verbal clues to the importance of ideas and the relationships among points.

Even when students' notes are sketchy, several studies indicated that students achieved more on tests when they had their own notes to review. Mary Ann Rafoth found that even if students did not review their notes before a test, they still did better than those who did not take notes at all. Those who took notes and reviewed did better yet (Rafoth et al., 1993, p. 123). Clearly, taking notes aids recall and comprehension.

Rafoth emphasizes the importance of teaching note-taking strategies and suggests the following for improving students' skills:

1. *Skeletal notes:* For complicated material, skeletal notes provide a framework. The basic outline is provided, with blank spaces for students to fill in. The more space provided, the more students write. The framework helps students organize material.

2. *Instructor's notes:* Some teachers provide a complete set of notes to students, but researchers report that students remember their own notes much better. Students may not understand the teacher-written notes.

3. *Note-taking cues:* Putting notes on the board and using particular words and phrases help students to know when and what to write. For example, a teacher might say, "The reason that . . ." or "There are three causes for . . ." or "An important finding was . . ." (Rafoth et al., 1993, p. 128).

4. *Transparencies:* Rafoth cautions about the use of transparencies because often the information is too complex and should be previewed before it is presented on transparencies. Because students have to listen and read during the lecture, it is difficult for them to take notes.

5. *Note-taking reviews:* Teachers should periodically collect students' notes, review them, and make suggestions for improvement. The suggestions need to be specific (not just tell them to take more notes). The notes are not evaluated for a grade.

6. *Organization and elaboration:* Encourage students not only to read their notes over but also to organize and classify the information. This helps them understand and remember. Rafoth cautions that students should not attempt to relate lecture material to previous knowledge while taking notes but should do so later (1993, p. 124).

7. *Using a split page:* Students divide a page in half vertically and use the left side for the major points and the right for supporting ideas. This helps them to recognize major points and facilitates their self-study when reviewing notes.

When viewing a film or video, students follow the same procedures as those for listening to lectures. The teacher may direct the students' attention to particular scenes or areas of importance before they watch the film. For example, a teacher may want students to be aware of the characters' conflicting values or of influences that shape behavior and outcomes. As with lectures, students should not take notes during the viewing, although they may want to jot down a pertinent word or date. Immediately after the film, students write what they think is important to remember and then share what they have written with others in a small group, making additions or changes where appropriate.

Note-Taking from Reading

Students need instruction on how to select, organize, and synthesize information from reading, particularly in recognizing the main idea (Washington, 1988, p. 24). Advance organizers, like the split page suggested by Rafoth, help students search for main topics and look for supporting evidence. Students may have trouble deciding what they should write down and often copy verbatim.

A variation of the method for lecture notes is useful for taking notes from reading material. As a modeling strategy, a teacher could prepare an overhead of a paragraph from the textbook. After it is read aloud, the teacher turns the overhead off and asks what students believe should be jotted down as notes. The teacher records the suggestions and discusses how notes reflect the information, but in the reader's own words.

To help students understand the importance of brevity but thoroughness in note-taking, the teacher shares a paragraph, then shows them an example of notes that essentially copy all the material, followed by an example of sketchy, incomplete notes. Through discussion, the teacher explains the need to avoid copying the author's exact words, but to record enough information to help the reader remember what was read. With repeated practice, students learn how to take notes on important points and to paraphrase rather than write the author's words verbatim.

Regie Routman suggests that after students have written notes from material they read, the teacher collects the notes, not to grade or even read but simply to put aside. A few days later, the teacher hands the notes back to the students, who write a paragraph or two based solely on their own notes. This exercise is a good check for the students themselves to see if their note-taking is adequate (Routman, 1991, p. 284).

Writing notes from the material they are reading works better than highlighting the text, for two reasons. One is that, by the actual act of writing notes, the student is learning; second, because the notes are in the student's own words, some comprehension is taking place. Students occasionally highlight an entire paragraph or page and avoid making decisions about what is the important information. Also, by highlighting, the students focus only on the exact words of the text rather than paraphrasing the material into their own words. Little learning results from this method, either at the time of reading or when studying for an exam.

The more one engages in thinking about the text, the more learning occurs. In *How Writing Shapes Thinking*, Judith Langer and Arthur Applebee explain that the more content is manipulated, the more likely students will be to remember and understand it. Any kind of written response leads to more learning than reading without writing (Langer & Applebee, 1987, p. 130).

Note-taking follows four steps:

1. Listening, viewing, or reading carefully
2. Writing notes based on the lecture, film, or text
3. Sharing notes with other students in a small group
4. Adding information gained from the discussion to one's own notes.

Graphic Organizers

Graphic organizers are useful in both reading and lecture note-taking. In either situation, teachers need to give an overview of the organizers before the students use them. Cathy Sakta, a university instructor, explains that using graphic organizers helps students to listen more effectively and include essential information. The structure teaches students how to focus on main ideas and supporting details (Sakta, 1992, p. 482). Teachers can gradually reduce the amount of information provided on the organizers until the students do not use them at all. To achieve this independence, Sakta suggests the following plan: (p. 484)

1. First, have students use the complete organizer, including topics, main ideas, and essential details arranged in the order in which students hear them in lecture or read them from texts.
2. Next, supply only the topics and the main ideas, leaving numbered spaces for the supporting details.
3. Give the topic and the main ideas, but omit the number and placement of the details.
4. Only the topic is provided, and spaces are left for the remaining information.

Many educators have designed graphic organizers, which differ in structure, but they all focus on major points and supporting details. Some include provisions for connecting the notes with prior knowledge. A few examples are included here.

Smith and Tompkins suggest organizers with layouts to suggest relationships among the details. For example, if the reading involves a cause–effect relationship, the note-taking might look like Figure 5–1.

Christen and Murphy, in a handbook written for secondary students, propose a graphic organizer (Figure 5–2) that has students determine the main idea, select important details, and then write a summary. Writing the summary helps students to see if they understand the material (Christen & Murphy, 1992, p. 60).

The purpose of graphic organizers is to guide students into taking adequate notes, not to insist that they fill out teacher-prepared forms. The guides should not be evaluated at all; an occasional read-through by a teacher will determine if a student is on the right track. We want to help students become independent in

FIGURE 5-1 Note-Taking Showing a
Cause–Effect Relationship

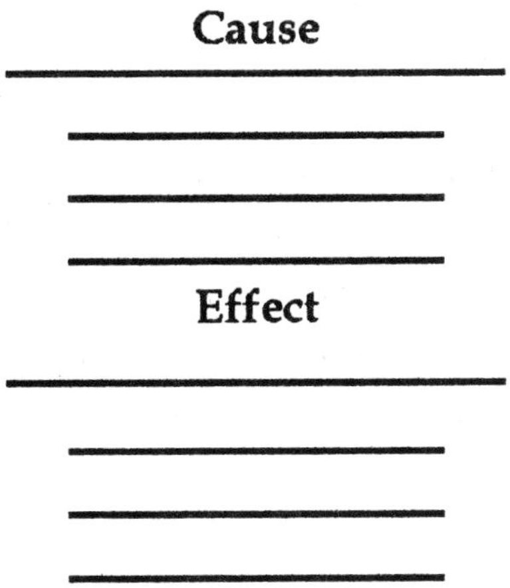

Cause

_____

_____

_____

_____

Effect

_____

_____

_____

_____

FIGURE 5-2 Graphic Organizer

their learning and studying; the notes they take are for them to use, not an assignment to satisfy the teacher.

Developing Questions

Writing notes is an excellent way for students to discover if they have questions. Only when they put information into their own words will it be obvious to them that they may not understand a particular point or concept.

In recent years, teachers have made serious efforts to improve their own questioning abilities. They now ask students questions that involve more higher order thinking than simple recall ones; also, teachers wait longer after asking a question to allow time for students to think. But what about students developing questions on their own to facilitate their learning? As with the other strategies discussed in this chapter, the more students are actively involved in their own learning, the more they learn and the longer the information is retained.

Peter Gray explains a method developed by Marcia Heiman to help college students get more out their education. The strategies she used are adaptable for high school classes as well. "The most striking finding was that successful students engage in a mental dialogue with authors and lectures" (Gray, 1993, p. 70). The dialogue is created by the students asking questions, and then seeking the answers from the readings and lectures. Heiman tells students that unless they know the questions the readings and lectures are attempting to answer, they will not understand the material. She taught students a method to use when reading their textbooks. The method is outlined here, but adapted for secondary students:

1. Skim the reading by section, read all the captions, and infer the section's main questions
2. Write out the questions.
3. Read carefully to discover the answers to the questions.
4. If necessary, change the questions to more closely fit the information. (Gray, 1993, p. 71)

Students found that the questions helped to keep them focused on the reading.

Gray also had his students write out questions that the readings raised, but did not answer. He wanted students to question the validly and inherent value of an author's statements (1993, p. 72). This suggestion is especially helpful when students are reading texts that are persuasive in nature—for example, advertisements, political arguments, and essays written on topical social issues. Even students of middle school age can discern biases when they are taught to examine the evidence presented in making claims. For this age group, advertisements work well, but older high school students can be successful with quite sophisticated material. Using such an approach helps students not only to read better but also to become better informed citizens and consumers.

Alison King suggests using generic self-questions with students to help them process the information in a lecture:

What is the main idea?
How does _____ relate to _____ ?
Do I agree or disagree?
How is this related to what we studied earlier?
What conclusions can I draw?

She found that using the generic questions as guides helped students ask higher order questions and elaborate more in their responses (King, 1992, p. 305). Both comprehension and recall improved using this method.

Summarizing and Paraphrasing

Summarizing means to capture the "gist of a piece as well as reduce the material substantially" (King, 1992, p. 305). To involve students in increasing comprehension and recall through summarizing, they need to generate their own sentences rather than copy ones they have read or heard. Summarizing makes students more apt to relate the new information to what they already know—in other words, their prior knowledge. To guide students in writing summaries, King suggests using a scheme they can follow. First, students write the topic of the lecture or passage using one sentence that reflects the main idea. This is followed by one subtopic and its related ideas, then the next subtopic, and so on through the material (King, 1992, p. 311). In this way, the topics are linked together, which makes them easier to understand and remember. Summaries should not include the reader's opinions.

Writing summaries helps students focus on the material and develop the habit of close reading. At times it is appropriate to skim material to get a general idea of what it is about, but we also want students to know when and how to read with close attention, especially when reading highly technical material.

Writing Reports and Research Papers

Because of the connections among the study strategies reviewed in this chapter and these longer writing assignments, a generic overview of helping students write successful reports is given here. Writing term papers, reports, or research papers is appropriate for many, if not all, content areas. Examples of research papers and reports are suggested in the subject-related chapters and in the final chapter on interdisciplinary units. Regardless of the content, teachers can use the same approach. Although many students have difficulty in writing these longer assignments, by following the method described here even students of lower ability can successfully locate information and write a well-organized report.

Selecting Topics

To begin a successful project, students need latitude in choosing their own topic. The more freedom they have in deciding what they will write about, the more interest they have in the topic. Teachers have parameters on topic choices, but keeping them as open as possible ensures greater student involvement. Selecting a topic does not have to be an isolated activity. After the teacher explains the assignment and provides suggestions and ideas, students choose one or more topics to work on. Then they meet in small groups to discuss their ideas and help each other clarify and narrow their choices. Meeting with others at the very beginning of the project helps students gain a sense of what others are doing and a better idea of what they may choose as a viable topic.

Using Prior Knowledge

The next step is for students to write everything they already know about the topic. This is a level 1 writing activity, so they are free to write in any manner that works for them. They may use a loosely organized narrative style, mapping, clustering, or a list. The objective is to get as much information down as possible so that students are not beginning a report from a void but, rather, from a wealth of information. Teachers encourage students to add information they may not be positive about and then to insert a question mark to indicate they need to check on that information. Students continually add to the material and shape it into more organized information.

Developing Questions

The next step is for students to look over what they have written, decide where they need to gather more information, and write questions to be answered. Developing questions is of primary importance. Too often students begin a report with only a general sense of what information they are trying to find. It is difficult to find something when you do not know what you are looking for. Students who go to the library with only a vague idea of what they are looking for spend their time unproductively. Beginning library work with only a general topic in mind—whether it be a particular element, inventor, author, country, or animal, or a subject such as electricity, muscles, or the Civil War—does not provide enough guidance for students to locate appropriate information successfully in a reasonable amount of time. Students become frustrated, especially those who struggle with writing. When students develop questions that need to be answered, they know better where to find the resources and, furthermore, can recognize the answer when they read it.

Preparing to Gather Reference Material

Once the students decide on what questions they will use to guide the report, they write each question on an individual sheet of paper. If they have four questions, they use four sheets. In addition, they title another sheet, headed "References." References do not have to be located only in the library. Many teachers unnecessarily limit the types of resources, rather than encouraging students to find a variety of sources (Maxwell & Meiser, 1993, p. 133). Robert Perrin of

Indiana State University explains there are many untapped, but rich, sources for students to use.

> Students should look everywhere and explore every potential source of information. Why shouldn't students use interviews, both personal and telephone? Why shouldn't students conduct surveys when the results would be enlightening? Why shouldn't students use personal experiences when it is appropriate? Why shouldn't students use films, pamphlets, lecture notes, records, or television programs when they supply helpful ideas, insights, and information? (Perrin, 1987, p. 51)

Using a variety of resources shifts the emphasis from library work for the purpose of using the library to finding information that results in an interesting and informative report or project.

Gathering Information

As students locate a reference, they jot down the bibliography information on the sheet titled "References" and number each entry. As they discover answers to their questions, they write the answers on the appropriate sheet. The first reference might provide information on two of the questions; students would write a 1 showing the resource and the information on one question sheet, then a 1 and the information for another question. They do not repeat the reference citation on the question sheets because the number refers them back to the reference sheet. Students add page numbers next to the notes, but nothing more. A second reference might answer another question, as well as add to one that already has notes. Figure 5–3 illustrates the appearance of the pages as the work progresses. If students write the notes on the question sheet and keep track of where they acquired the information, the notes follow an organizational scheme.

Drafting

With this method, all the notes pertaining to one area appear in one place. When students begin drafting, they do not search frantically through note cards trying to organize the material as they write. The original questions serve as headings for their report. Many students use the question itself as a heading, while others turn it into a statement; either way is appropriate.

Using this method helps all students, but especially those who are disorganized or who are overwhelmed by the prospect of a long writing assignment. On large projects that require blocks of time, structure helps writers focus on what they need to do next and what they have accomplished.

Summary

Teaching students how to use writing as a study skill helps them become independent learners, a lifelong survival skill. The more interaction students have with the material they study, the more they comprehend and retain.

FIGURE 5-3   Reference List in Process

Therefore, taking notes, summarizing, and developing questions are ways for them to become more efficient learners. Teachers can provide activities to teach these skills as well as adapt their own teaching behavior to facilitate the students' success.

Discussion Questions

1. How can teachers use their knowledge of writing to help students learn?
2. In what ways do questions serve as a prereading focus?
3. When is memorizing important in learning and when is it not?
4. How does writing develop thinking skills?
5. What does it mean to be an independent learner?

Suggested Activities

1. Select a research topic from the content you will be teaching and devise discovery activities to use with your future secondary students that will help them become interested in the topic.
2. Select passages from a secondary textbook that you could use for teaching students note-taking.
3. Develop questions based on readings you are doing for courses.
4. Choose a topic you might be asked to write about and, using prior knowledge, write everything you can think of about the subject.

5. Using your information from the previous activity, read over what you wrote and devise several questions you need to answer in order to write a well-thought-out and interesting report.

References

Applebee, Arthur. *Writing in the Secondary School.* Urbana, IL: National Council of Teachers of English, 1981.

Britton, James. "Writing-and-Reading in the Classroom." In Anne Haas Dyson, ed., *Collaboration through Writing and Reading* (pp. 217–246). Urbana, IL: National Council of Teachers of English, 1989.

Christen, William, & Thomas Murphy. *Smart Learning: A Study Skills Guide for Teens.* Bloomington, IN: Grayson Bernard, 1992.

Dana, Carol, & Margaret Rodriquez. "TOAST: A System to Study Vocabulary." *Reading Research and Instruction*, 1992, 31(4), pp. 78–84.

Gere, Anne Ruggles, ed. *Roots in the Sawdust.* Urbana, IL: National Council of Teachers of English, 1985.

Gray, Peter. "Engaging Students' Intellects: The Immersion Approach to Critical Thinking in Psychology Instruction." *Teaching of Psychology, 20,*(2), April 1993, pp. 68–74.

King, Alison. "Comparison of Self-Questioning, Summarizing, and Note-taking–Review as Strategies for Learning from Lectures." *American Educational Research Journal, 29*(2), Summer 1992, pp. 303–323.

Langer, Judith A., & Arthur Applebee. *How Writing Shapes Thinking.* Urbana, IL: National Council of Teachers of English, 1987.

Maxwell, Rhoda J., & Mary Meiser. *Teaching English in Middle and Secondary Schools.* New York: Macmillan, 1993.

Perrin, Robert. "Myths about Research." *English Journal*, November 1987, pp. 50–53.

Pohve, Thomas J. "Beyond Location: Using Graphic Organizers to Initiate Comprehension in the Library Media Program." *School Library Media Activities Monthly, 7*(1), September 1990, pp. 31–32.

Potts, Bonnie. "Improving the Quality of Student Notes." *ERIC/AE Digest*, U.S. Department of Education, October 1993.

Rafoth, Mary Ann, et al. *Strategies for Learning and Remembering: Study Skills Across the Curriculum.* Washington, DC: National Education Association, 1993.

Routman, Regie. *Invitations.* Portsmouth, NH: Heinemann, 1991.

Sakta, Cathy G. "The Graphic Organizer: A Blueprint for Taking Lecture Notes." *Journal of Reading, 35*(6), March 1992, pp. 482–484.

Smith, Patricia L., & Gail Tompkins. "Structured Notetaking: A New Strategy for Content Area Readers." *Journal of Reading, 32*(1), October 1988, pp. 46–52.

Washington, Valerie M. "Report Writing: A Practical Application of Semantic Mapping." *Teacher Educator, 24*(1), Summer 1988, pp. 24–30.

6

IMPROVING WRITING SKILLS

Unarguably, writing must ultimately be respectful of conventions. Punctuation and capitalization are not just mechanisms for assuring writing's clarity; they also amount to a symbolic commitment to orthodoxy—a way of establishing one's intention to honor the forms of rightness that others have long agreed about. But, much as grammar shouldn't be taught as writing, neither should correctness be taught as non-writing, as a set of arcane rules absorbable only through endless sets of drills.
—PETER STILLMAN, 1984

Prereading Questions

1. With what areas of writing skills might you have problems? How have you learned to improve your writing skills?

2. With what writing skills do you think students in secondary schools might have the most difficulty?

3. At what point in the writing process should writing skills be taught?

4. Who in the schools should have the responsibility for helping students improve their writing?

5. How would helping students improve their writing in chemistry be the same as and/or different from conducting a social studies class?

Introduction

Because we use writing throughout the curriculum, helping students improve their writing becomes part of every classroom. Content-area teachers, other than English teachers, concentrate on the skills important for teaching and learning their particular subjects. They want students to write well for the writing they assign, but they are not looking for a wide range of improvement overall. Although teachers may be frustrated with students' writing problems, they do not want— indeed, cannot—spend too much time working on skills. If the skills are taught within the process of writing, however, and if the responsibility of learning the skills rests with the students, much can be accomplished in all subject areas.

Teaching writing skills does not require an extended amount of time or effort for teachers. Skills are best taught with specificity; that is, one should teach the skills students need because of the writing assignments in the class. Also, teachers need to remember that writing conventions change just as language itself changes. We do not need to be overzealous about the finer points of punctuation and grammar.

Levels of Writing

The level of writing skills expected for an assignment and the purpose of the assignment go hand in hand. As discussed in the chapter on writing levels, the type of writing depends on the teacher's purpose or reason for planning the activity. If a teacher wants students to reflect on and respond to a lecture or readings, the appropriate level is 1; for homework and most of the writing assigned, the level is 2; only an occasional project or report should be at level 3. This classification affects how closely student writing will reflect formal standards.

Level 1 often consists of written-down thoughts, disorganized and expressed in incomplete sentences. Even commonly used words may be misspelled at level 1. The most common punctuation mark is the dash, representing how one's mind works. This lack of conformity to conventions is not only accepted but even encouraged so that the flow of thoughts is not disrupted.

Level 2 adheres more closely to conventional standards of spelling, punctuation, and organization. Teachers expect and evaluate for correct spelling of commonly used words, complete sentences, and a level of punctuation that fits students' grade level.

Level 3, formal writing, requires careful consideration of correct punctuation, spelling, and organization. Few if any errors should be present, but that varies by grade level and what teachers can realistically expect of their students.

Common Errors

Obviously, not all students make the same errors, but a few errors occur in student writing with consistent regularity, regardless of the subject or grade level. Teachers may want to teach short lessons and provide some practice on these particular items. In secondary schools, the following ten areas seem to cause the most confusion for student writers. The items are not in order of priority.

1. Using a plural pronoun with a singular noun
2. Knowing when to use *that, which, who*

3. Using colons
4. Using correct pronoun case
5. Punctuating compound sentences
6. Using commas
7. Changing voice inappropriately
8. Hyphening adjectives
9. Overusing nonspecific words (e.g., *very, so, nice*)
10. Using details and examples to support claims

Because these problems occur with regularity, teaching a short lesson on each one throughout the course is a benefit for students.

These lessons are about ten minutes long and are sometimes referred to as minilessons. The following description of a minilesson serves as a model for a beginning teacher.

First, the teacher explains that this particular problem occurs frequently in student papers. Then, using the overhead or board, the teacher provides several examples of correct ways to use the particular skill. For example, when teaching when to use a colon, one could first explain that the common mistake is to use a colon after an incomplete sentence, usually after a verb. A person may write incorrectly, "There are many reasons to study biology. They are: (reasons are listed)." The correct way is to place the colon after the word *biology.* "There are many reasons to study biology: (reasons are listed)." The students can suggest additional ways to use colons correctly. It is important not to expand the lesson with exercises that students complete. By using their own writing, students learn the skill within a context they will use.

Teachers should not follow a lesson with a sheet of examples that need to be corrected. An exercise is limited to a specific group of problems. "Such preidentification of possible errors doesn't exist when students do their own writing" (Belanoff, Rorschach, & Oberlink, 1993, p. xi). A teacher wants the colon to be used correctly in the student's *own* writing, and doing it out of the context of writing is ineffective. A student tutor, commenting on her tutee, wrote in her tutoring journal, "The problem with going over exercises is that he focuses on getting the right answer and not on understanding the concept" (Kendra Forest).

Errors from student papers should *never* be used as examples. Even with the student's name removed, the situation is extremely embarrassing and interferes with a student's self-esteem, an important element in developing a healthy learning environment.

Following the lesson, the students write an explanation and description of using the skill area they have just covered to keep in their writing folder or subject notebook as a reference. Once the skill is presented, student writing should reflect the correct use, which can then be part of the evaluation for level 3 assignments and perhaps for level 2, depending on the grade level.

The ten skills listed come from my classes and are not meant to be universal. However, first-year teachers may find the list helpful until they compile their own list of frequent misuses of writing skills.

When to Teach Writing Skills

Writing skills should be taught throughout the writing process: in the drafting stage, in the revising and editing stages, and after the evaluation. While students are working on drafting, teachers can present a lesson or two from the common errors list, plus areas that pertain to the particular assignment. Short lessons, to the point and related to the writing the students are currently doing, have more impact and success than skills taught out of context.

During the revising period, a teacher may notice particular areas of difficulty; that is the time to go over a skill with the whole class. During a peer editing session, problems with punctuation, spelling, and word usage become apparent; again, this is the time to help individuals and the class as a whole.

Students may also be having trouble with skills related to content, such as supporting evidence, clearly stated thesis, or including enough detail. An effective way to help students recognize where they need to add more detail and support is to have them outline their own papers. Objectivity is important; if students have difficulty with this, have them outline each other's papers. The process of outlining shows the gaps where they need to add additional material.

One way to keep track of students' problems is to use a skills sheet that lists the skills on the left side and has a grid on the right. Students' names are at the top of the grid if a teacher wants to keep track of errors for individual students. Otherwise, the teacher checks problem areas when grading papers without concern over each student. Teachers are looking for patterns. The skill sheet is most useful for showing when a writing skill needs to become the subject of a minilesson. An example of a skills sheet is illustrated in Figure 6–1. The skills listed depend on the subject, age level, and teacher.

FIGURE 6-1   Skills Sheet, Second Hour Class

	(Could list student names here)							
Not enough details and explanations								
Organization not clear								
Thesis not strong and clear								
Comma errors								
Semicolon errors								
Punctuation in general								
Underlining and quotations								
Plural verbs with singular subjects								

After the paper is evaluated by the teacher and returned to the student, students can review any problems they had with writing skills. A teacher can require students to analyze their own papers for problem areas, then make a list of areas to which they think they have to pay attention. By making their own lists, students become responsible for their own improvement. The list goes into their writing folder or notebook, and they refer to it the next time they revise and edit a paper. A self-generated list is much more helpful than an editing or proofreading list from a textbook or from a teacher. These are items the students themselves believe they need to work on or be more aware of.

Vocabulary and Spelling

Each discipline has its own specialized vocabulary that teachers want students to understand and use. Vocabulary is important because it gives students a way of talking about each subject in specific ways that help them understand the subject. Learning how to spell words and learning the meaning of words are not always the same. Spelling is a skill needed in writing, whereas vocabulary is important in speaking, listening, reading, and writing. The study of words in relation to a particular discipline involves both spelling and vocabulary.

Words unfamiliar to the students should be introduced in the context of a unit of study, not in isolation. Unless we see and use a word fairly often, it is difficult to remember. When words are explained, they are best remembered if a teacher writes them on the board, pronounces them, and has the students write them into their notebooks. If appropriate, the root words and the historical significance of each word are explained. In science, for example, words often come from people's names or from Greek and Latin roots. Learning about words rather than having a list of words to memorize helps students appreciate "the rich, complex fabric of language—its properties, uses, and historical development" (Hodges, 1982, p. 13). Such an approach helps students understand and remember the words.

Only when students are expected to use the new words in writing do they need to be concerned with spelling, and even then only if the writing is at level 2 or 3. If a teacher wants students to use words that are new to them, the best approach is simply to write the words on the board so that spelling is not a problem. If the word is one that will come up often, then students should learn to spell it correctly. For words used only within a short unit of study, however, although they need to know their meanings, they do not need to know how to spell them. For some students, spelling is a difficult skill, and we do not want to emphasize spelling when it is unnecessary. Overemphasis on spelling detracts from learning content by taking up an undue amount of time and effort.

Handbooks

Writers' handbooks are essential for everyone who writes. Too often, however, they are used inappropriately as textbooks, especially in English classes, instead of as reference books. Every student needs to own or at least have ready access to such a handbook. It is best when teachers of all subjects in a school agree on which handbook to use and have a class set in every classroom. Even without such agreement, every teacher needs to provide an up-to-date handbook for students to use, just as dictionaries are available for students.

In choosing a handbook, the first section to examine is the index. Because the handbook is a reference tool, it is essential that information be easy to locate. An index that breaks down a subject into increments is easiest for students to use. For example, in one handbook there are 24 entries under quotations that help students find what they need quickly (*Bedford Guide*); another has a specific entry for *"till, until"* (*St. Martin's Handbook*); a third has an extensive section under diction (*The Allyn and Bacon Handbook*). The examples of correct usage should be clear and easy to understand.

A teacher would want to read the section on documentation carefully, making sure that the explanations are easy to follow and that several examples are included. Using documentation correctly is difficult regardless of the style. Because the handbooks are used across curricular areas, it is helpful if three systems of documentation are included: MLA (Modern Language Association), APA (American Psychological Association), and CBE (Council of Biology Editors). Depending on the subject, a teacher may want to use a style not included in a general handbook and will need to provide a style sheet for students that covers that particular documentation. Law, geology, chemistry, medicine, mathematics, and physics all have professional style manuals (Troyka, 1993, p. 644).

Learning how to use documentation is not easy, and students will need practice before working on an assignment that requires documenting references. One activity that works well is to have students work together in small groups and write a short report on an issue related to the current topic being discussed in class. The emphasis should be on finding and referencing several sources. Writing summaries of the references is adequate. Because the purpose of the assignment is to provide practice in finding and citing references, the paper would be a level 2, and the evaluation would focus on the documentation style. It is not necessary that students memorize a style sheet; rather, we want students to know where to find examples of correct documentation and to use one consistently.

Providing students with examples of published papers from the course content helps them to understand how to use the various styles. "The papers will make students aware that there is no single right way to cite sources; there is, instead, a way that is appropriate for a particular writing task and audience" (Troyka, 1993, p. 691). Our job is to give students ample opportunities to practice using an appropriate style.

Summary

Content-area teachers need to teach the writing skills that pertain to the assignments they develop for the students. They do not have to put heavy emphasis on the skills but should teach them in the context of the students' writing. The purpose of each assignment determines the appropriate level of writing skills. When teachers across the curriculum work together on designing writing activities, then students will come to realize writing is important in every class.

Discussion Questions

1. What writing skills are unique or are emphasized in writing for the content area you will teach?
2. Why do different disciplines use different documentation styles?
3. What areas of writing skills cause you the most difficulty?
4. How is teaching writing skills similar to and different from teaching the skills needed in other disciplines?
5. How can we encourage students to take responsibility for using acceptable writing skills?

Suggested Activities

1. Review several professional journals in your teaching area and determine what documentation style they use. Also, analyze the general style of writing: length of paragraphs, number of lists, examples, tone, and diction.
2. Make a list of writing skills that you want to focus on for your own writing.
3. Working in groups, write short lessons for teaching one or more skills to a middle or high school class.
4. Interview a teacher of middle or high school students to determine what he or she thinks are the biggest problems in student writing.
5. Read a chapter in a student textbook and decide what vocabulary you think would be appropriate for students to learn. Which of these words should they know how to spell?

References

Belanoff, Pat, Betsy Rorschach, & Mia Oberlink. *The Right Handbook,* 2nd ed. Portsmouth, NH: Boynton/Cook, 1993.

Hacker, Diana. *The Bedford Handbook for Writers,* 3rd ed. Boston: Bedford Books, St. Martin's Press, 1991.

Hodges, Richard H. *Improving Spelling and Vocabulary in the Secondary School.* Urbana, IL: National Council Teachers of English, 1982.

Lunsford, Andrea, & Robert Connors. *The St. Martin's Handbook,* 2nd ed. New York: St. Martin's Press, 1992.

Rosen, Leonard J., & Laurence Behrens. *The Allyn and Bacon Handbook.* Boston: Allyn and Bacon, 1992.

Stillman, Peter. *The Why, What, and How of Writing Your Way.* Upper Montclair, NJ: Boynton/Cook, 1984.

Troyka, Lynn Quitman. *Simon & Schuster Handbook for Writers,* 3rd ed. Englewood Cliffs, NJ: Prentice-Hall, 1993.

7

WRITING IN MATH AND SCIENCE

Visualization is necessary for learning scientific and mathematical concepts. Although writing cannot replace it, visualization alone is not enough. Writing enables and enhances the intuition that science and math depend upon for understanding and progress. Good scientists and mathematicians write well.
—DALE WORSLEY & BERNADETTE MAYER, 1989, p. 3

Prereading Questions

1. How might writing enhance visualization in science and math?
2. In what ways have you used writing in science and math?
3. What connections might exist between writing in an English class and writing in science and math classes?
4. How does writing in math and science help students improve their writing?
5. Why would science and math teachers incorporate writing into their curriculum?

Introduction

Writing in science and writing in math are combined in one chapter because of the similarities in technical language and the importance of facts and concepts. Writing in math and science differs from writing in other curriculum areas in several ways. First, the vocabulary is specialized and, to many students, unfamiliar. Understanding the concepts requires close attention to details. Both depend on the ability to form questions as a learning process. Also, science and math call for abstract thinking, an ability many students have not fully developed.

In many important ways, however, writing in math and the sciences is similar to writing in the language arts. The attention to details is essential. To report observational data correctly, a scientist must use specific words and concrete images, just as one does in narrative writing. The reader must be able to picture in the mind's eye exactly what the writer sees. In math, sequence is vitally important as it is in narrative writing. Again, the reader must follow the sequence of events in the same way the writer understands them. Because of the similarities, writing taught in English is beneficial to writing in technological and scientific areas, and writing abilities learned in science and math benefit students' writing in other classes.

Types of Writing

The levels of writing are appropriate in science and math writing just as they are in all subjects. We write to think and think to write; therefore, much of our writing is putting thoughts on paper, not final drafts. For example, as mentioned in an earlier chapter, journals are important in any content area because students need to explore possibilities and connections among what they know, what they are discovering, and what they want to find out. Using level 1 writing helps students comprehend, remember, and develop critical thinking because they are concentrating on what they are discovering and learning, not on the mechanics of writing. Level 2 writing is appropriate for homework assignments, responses to readings, summaries of textbook chapters, or any writing where we want students to use conventional forms of writing but not spend the time to produce a polished product. Rather, the writing should focus on the understandings and connections. Level 3 is reserved for those special occasions when an error-free paper is absolutely required.

Math Writing Activities

Many students could better understand and use mathematics if we gave them more opportunities to write about and talk about the subject. Writing is a tool for learning that mathematics teachers have long overlooked.—JUDITH SALEM, 1982, p. 124

Math teachers who use writing in their classrooms find that students become actively engaged in their own learning. Pam Walpole, a high school math teacher, believes that writing and math go very well together: "Mathematics is a language itself; I encourage students to let their mastery of the English language help them master math" (Walpole, 1987, p. 51). More and more math teachers are incorporating writing into their teaching. Joan Countryman explains why: "We need to create situations where students can be active, creative and responsive to the physical world, and writing is an ideal activity for such a process" (1993, p. 51). Although many math teachers have used writing for some time, the National Council of Teachers of Mathematics (NCTM) brought increased emphasis to the importance of students learning how to communicate mathematics when the council published its new standards in 1989. The standards move instruction away from the recall of terminology and routine manipulation of symbols. Students must be able to describe how they arrived at an answer and the difficulties they may have had. The focus should be on the students' own language; opportunities for discussion help students make connections between mathematics and society. Countryman explains that "students need opportunities to organize, interpret and explain; to construct, symbolize and communicate; to plan, infer and reflect" (1993, p. 51). Examples of how some math teachers go about achieving these goals are explained here.

Communicating in Math

The NCTM standards stress communication because students need to "construct links between their informal, intuitive notions and the abstract language and symbolism of mathematics . . ." (Fortescue, 1994, p. 26). Don Schmidt, a junior high school teacher, uses writing "mainly as a way of opening lines of communication" when teaching math (Schmidt, 1985, p. 104). One way he achieves this is to have his students write "admit slips" on which they are free to express how they feel about the math assignments or math in general. The slips are anonymous, and Schmidt reads them aloud in class to give students an opportunity to hear how others are doing and what they are thinking. The activity helps students realize they are not alone in having difficulty understanding a particular assignment or in feeling overwhelmed with the present work: "Problems that can be verbalized can be discussed; they become something that can be attacked and handled" (Schmidt, 1985, p. 106). Students use admit slips to share successes as well as problems or frustrations. Giving students opportunities to write during class time provides time for them to reflect on their math learning experiences. Knowing that they have an audience for their concerns builds a sense of a learning community.

Journals are also useful for communication between student and teacher. As students work on math problems, they jot down in their journals where they have difficulty. They need to keep the journal handy and to write as they work so that they record immediate concerns rather than trying to remember later where and when they had trouble. If they cannot finish a problem, they work on it as far as they can and record where they are stumped. The students turn the journals in with the assigned work. Teachers quickly scan them to look for problems the students have experienced. Depending on how frequently a particular problem occurs, the teacher then may work with individual students, work with a small group, or present explanations to the whole class. The information gathered from the journals suggests to a teacher what to review with the class or what concepts are not clear. If a teacher asks a class if anyone had difficulty with the assignment, few students are willing to speak up. However, by writing questions and frustrations in a journal, privacy is maintained, and a teacher can provide the specific help a student needs.

Mark Wagler encourages teachers to have their students read and write math. He required his students to write articles for *It Figures*, a publication by and for young mathematicians. Writing the articles helped increase the students' depth of inquiry: "As they listened, during journal time, to other students reading excerpts from drafts of their articles, they began to believe more strongly in their capacity for solving difficult problems. As they wrestled with their own writing, their mathematical ideas became more precise and coherent" (Wagler, 1993, p. 92).

Every student has a "math history." If teachers ask students to write their math history early in the year, they will learn a great deal about the students' sense of self-esteem and willingness to learn math. Such information contributes to how teachers approach their teaching. Learning about past experiences is helpful in any subject, but especially in math. Many students have the idea that math is difficult, which can be a barrier to learning. Knowing how students feel about math helps teachers plan ways to encourage their self-concept in math. It helps, too, by setting up a comfortable sharing between teacher and student.

Writing Explanations

Joan Countryman writes "that to learn mathematics, students must construct it for themselves" (1993, p. 51). One important way for students to construct meaning in math is to explain in writing how to solve a problem. The ability to explain how to solve a math problem shows greater understanding than getting the right answer. For instance, if students can explain how to multiply fractions, using details and specific examples, they can use that knowledge with any related problem.

Explaining math concepts in words helps students realize they may not fully understand even though they are able to do the problems. Without fully comprehending the concept, they tend to forget how to work the problems. By writing out the definitions and explanations, they can see exactly where their understanding breaks down and can then ask specific questions to gain the information. Whatever the current topic, students should practice writing out explanations, not necessarily using technical language but in their own words. A few examples follow:

1. Explain the difference between factors of a number and multiples of a number.
2. What does it mean to find the square root of a number?
3. How is the square root related to squaring a number?
4. What is the difference between an equation and an inequality?
5. What is a circumference? When would one need to know the measurement of a circumference?
6. Explain the function of a decimal point.

Another example of using prose to explain math comes when one writes two-column proofs in geometry. Russel Kenyon suggests that students write out their thoughts in prose and then examine and evaluate them. Once the students have tried the prose method, they are "usually able to organize information more effectively and meet with more success" than using the traditional two-column proof (Kenyon, 1989, p. 202).

Pam Walpole has her high school students write rulesheets where they explain the methods they used to solve problems. If they have misunderstood, the rulesheets allow her to notice and then to help them in specific ways. She explains that "Rulesheets also lead students to organize what they have learned, to make a conscious effort to look for patterns and to examine theory" (Walpole, 1987, p. 51). She encourages them to study from their own rulesheets rather than from the textbook. Her students find the rulesheets helpful. She quotes what one student wrote in an evaluation:

> Rulesheets saved the day—I really enjoyed doing them because you have to write them as though you're explaining it thoroughly to someone else—makes it easier to understand yourself. (Walpole, 1987, p. 53)

When evaluating the rulesheets, Walpole reads only for clear explanations and mathematical accuracy, which designates them as a level 2 writing assignment.

Narrative Writing

Narrative writing helps students think through their ideas and clarify their understanding. For example, writing a paragraph explaining how to organize information from a matrix helps students read and construct graphic representations of data.

Also, students may write a paragraph explaining the difference between factors of a number and multiples of a number; or explain the difference between squaring a number and taking the square root of a number.

Countryman suggests having students write a narrative account of a particular concept. Students may work problems correctly because they have memorized definitions but do not understand the meanings and cannot transfer the knowledge to other situations. As a solution to this problem, she outlines the following assignment:

Students describe the concept or problem in their own words, then explain their approach to solving the problem and what the solutions proved. They write a final paper including illustrations and examples (Countryman, 1993, p. 56).

Group Work

With the emphasis on speaking, listening, reading, and writing in learning math, group work becomes an integral part of any math classroom. The NCTM standards include encouraging teamwork so that students learn the value of working with others to achieve a goal. Karen D. Wood suggests that students be grouped heterogeneously so they learn from their experiences and can help one another (Wood, 1992, p. 97). She describes a group activity called a *reaction guide* used as a review session. Students work in small groups and complete the reaction guide, a list of statements about the topic that are either correct or incorrect. As a group, students check whether they agree or disagree with each statement and then explain why in writing. The group activity of discussing, reading, and writing helps them clear up any misconceptions they may have (Wood, 1992, p. 99).

Working in groups is especially helpful for problem solving. On their own, many students will become discouraged, but a group effort of discussing and thinking aloud keeps each one involved. The outcome needs to be in writing so that the students stay focused and come up with specific solutions (Wadlington, Bitner, Partridge, & Austin, 1992, p. 207).

As in other subjects, students learn from each other. To promote understanding, learners need to talk about math. One way to facilitate talking is to have small-group discussions concerning math homework. Students work together to solve problems and discuss any problems they encountered while working alone.

Math Vocabulary

To understand mathematics, students need to have knowledge of "both mathematics as a language and the language used to teach mathematics" (Miller, 1993, p. 311). Diane Miller cites a recent study done in Australia showing that students in the sample were unable to define mathematics vocabulary in their own language (Miller, 1993, p. 312). The study has implications for teaching math in this country as well. The words used in the study are common ones that we expect students to know—for example, *fraction, average, denominator,* and *digit.*

Miller suggests that teachers create activities that link mathematical concepts to the everyday world. For example, have students bring to school a variety of round objects; then, in small groups, the students measure and record in a table the circumferences and diameters of various circles. Students can then calculate decimal values for pi. With such an activity, students will relate the meaning of pi to a practical understanding. Miller explains that the "direct teaching of the specialized vocabulary of mathematics contributes to students' conceptual understanding of mathematics" (1993, p. 313). When students link aspects of the environment with math concepts, a sense of ownership arises. The ability to communicate knowledge about a concept, skill, or generalization is evidence of this ownership (Miller, 1993, p. 313). Students need to construct meaning, not memorize a formula.

Science Writing Activities

> *What I have discovered is that writing helps my students understand science more fully than any other teaching strategy can.*
> *—PATRICIA JOHNSON, HIGH SCHOOL SCIENCE TEACHER*

Genuine science—that is, what scientists do—is solving problems. Are the science experiments students do really problems to solve, or are they merely designed to show what the teacher wants them to know? If students are required to fill in blanks on a worksheet, they are not problem solving. Worksheets mean "right answers" and take the creativity out of science. Yet science can be the most creative of all our fields of study. We want students to think about science, not find "right answers." Writing can help achieve that goal.

Students in the United States rank near the bottom in studies of education performance. But as Rutherford and Ahlgren point out in *Science for All Americans* (1990, p. x1), the curriculum does not have to include more material. Rather, they suggest that teachers focus on a few key concepts. Teaching students ways of thinking and learning will help them acquire scientific knowledge more than teaching facts.

Students need to engage in meaningful talk about what they are reading in science, whether it is textbooks or other informational sources. Many students, especially if they have difficulty in reading, will have difficulty in reading science materials. Teachers need to help students learn how to read captions and section headings as aids to comprehension. Gaskins and colleagues explain that helping students learn how to write summaries in their own words, defend a point of view, and evaluate another's interpretation will aid in their understandings of content (1994, p. 559). These authors add that if students complete a brief written response based on the readings, they are more likely to participate in discussion (1994, p. 559).

In science as in other content areas, students need to use a variety of language functions: expressive, informative, and poetic. The writing activities need to include all three levels of writing. Expressive writing helps students understand and develop ideas in their science lessons. We need many different types of writing for learning science (Watts, 1984, p. 118).

There is a growing belief that science instruction must include process skills of observing, inferring, experimenting, and interpreting, rather than emphasize facts (Jones, 1994, p. 36). If students are provided with tools for learning, they can be "successful users and consumers of science" throughout their lives (p. 36). Writing helps students develop the process skills because they become actively involved in what they are learning, not passive receivers of information.

Acquiring science knowledge demands application of a variety of literacy skills because content information is rooted in written and oral language (Casteel & Isom, 1994, p. 538). The literacy skills of graphing, diagramming, recording, and reporting are important in organizing, analyzing, and publishing science data (p. 542). Incorporating these literacy skills in science teaching gives students a better understanding of science.

The more teachers can involve students in science class activities, the more students will learn and remember. James Scarnati has designed a unit for middle school that is activity-based. His reason for developing the activities is that "to read about an event is one thing, but to experience the event is immensely more meaningful" (Scarnati, 1994, p. 3) Writing activities are used throughout the unit because, as Scarnati explains, "to write well is to think well and to think well is to be able to solve problems, and that is what science is all about" (p. 3).

His unit is on the study of earthworms. To begin, he brings a box of earthworms into class, and students attempt to guess what "wild animal" is in the box by using their five senses. Then students observe the worms firsthand using a hand lens and rulers. They write their observations in notebooks and discuss what they have learned. Students then write ten questions they would like to ask an earthworm during an interview. The class is divided into two groups, with half taking the role of earthworms and the others acting as reporters. The students pair off, conduct the interviews, switch roles, and repeat the process.

For the final activity, the students write a feature newspaper article about earthworms. Scarnati reminds them of the four basic purposes for writing: to narrate, describe, explain, and persuade. He tells them to include all of these in the article. The unit is successful because students write best about what they experience directly.

Poetry in Science

One might not think of poetry as appropriate for science class, but teachers successfully incorporate poetry in several ways. Patricia Johnson, a high school teacher, uses poetry to help her students learn vocabulary. She asks students to write *biocrostics*, a version of the "biopoem." Students write the name of the plant or animal they are studying vertically on the paper, using the letters as the first letter of each line. Each line must include a fact about the plant or animal. Johnson explains that the higher level classes are required to use scientific nomenclature (Johnson, 1985, p. 93). The poems require students to know facts and understand vocabulary. A middle school student wrote the following poem when studying warm-blooded vertebrates:

> Wolves
> Or Canis Lupus, part of the Canidae family
> Live in woodland, stay in packs
> Vary in size, around 4 feet long
> Eat meat
> So they are called carnivores.
>   —Jessa Olien

One middle school teacher uses poetry in science as a final project. For instance, after a unit on volcanoes, the students wrote a poem explaining and describing volcanic eruptions. Poetry helps students develop their ability to record descriptions. Another poetry activity for middle school is included in a study of crystals. After students grow crystals and write their observations, they write a poem in the shape of their crystals. The poem describes a specific crystal.

A fourth suggestion for poetry in science comes from a study of habitat. Students choose an animal they want to write about and then write all they can think of describing the particular animal. To begin the poem, they look over their writing and choose one word that describes their selection. The next line is two words describing what the creature looks like. The third line is three words describing how the creature moves or where it lives. The fourth line is two words about how the animal contributes to the ecosystem or how it lives. The last line is another word that describes what the animal is.

Insect
Tiny, olive
Hop, fly, leaf
Herbivore, prey
Leafhopper
—Kris Schilling

Figurative language is not out of place in science because comparisons help a reader to visualize what the scientist is explaining.

Writing Detailed Descriptions

Detailed descriptions are of major importance to scientists. One activity that develops the ability to record observations carefully is a natural science project studying flowers. If possible, the teacher takes the students to a wooded area where they can study wildflowers in their natural habitat. Because the flowers are protected and cannot be picked, students bring paper and pencil to the site to describe the flowers in detail as well as to sketch them. Back in the classroom, where students must rely on their descriptions to identify the flowers, they discover that figurative language is helpful; comparisons work better than a general statement. For instance, "small" could mean any one of several sizes, but describing the blossom as about the size of a dime allows students to be specific.

The same results can be achieved by bringing nonprotected plants to the lab. The advantage of a field trip is that students can also describe the area where the flowers grow, noting shade, moisture, and terrain. They can use plant identification keys in the science lab to name each plant and then write a description of where it grows.

An additional activity that encourages careful observation and the recording of detailed descriptions requires group interaction. Each group of five to seven students receives a picture or series of pictures of a scientific phenomenon, such as a tornado funnel, ice storm, volcanic eruption, earthquake, or snowstorm. Each group writes a description of the events in the picture without stating what is happening. They use as many details as they want. Then the groups exchange papers and write a newspaper article explaining what has happened. All the groups share and discuss the results.

Writing Books for Younger Children

Explaining a concept or idea to someone else is a surefire way to know that one really understands. For this reason, and also to give students an opportunity to combine art and science while writing with a clear sense of audience, we designed a project for seventh-graders. The students write a book explaining some aspect of science to children in second grade.

To help our seventh-graders bridge the gap between creative writing and informational writing, we asked them to write informational books in a creative way (Maxwell & Judy, 1978). *Creative* is a nebulous term, but if we perceive it to mean combining information and ideas in new ways, looking for alternative explanations, using a novel approach for description, then the term *creative writing* should apply to *all* writing (Maxwell & Judy, 1978, p. 78). Too often, students equate report writing with a noncreative reporting of facts.

To guide students in creating books that are informationally sound and yet appealing to young readers, it is important to provide many examples of well-written science trade books intended for younger children. Secondary students may not have had opportunities to read the wealth of science literature now available. A few examples are *The Lady and the Spider* by Faith McNulty, *Disease Detectives* by Melvin Berger, and *Why Do Cats' Eyes Glow in the Dark* by Joanne Settel and Nancy Baggett, all discussed by Wendy Saul in *Vital Connections* (Saul & Jagusch, 1991, p. 11). The guidelines for successful science literature books that Saul describes provide guidance for the students as they write their books. She emphasizes the importance of correct information; a book that is beautifully and convincingly written but contains incorrect information is not an appropriate choice for young readers (Saul & Jagusch, 1991, p. 8). Students need to give the same care and respect to the truth in composing their books.

The project begins with a consideration of what makes a book interesting to read and also provides information to a reader. Students quickly catch on to the importance of illustrations, graphics, and descriptive language. To encourage a keen sense of audience, it helps to have the elementary and secondary students meet each other while the project is in progress. Schedules are always difficult to coordinate, but the payoff for students is tremendous. Interest in the project runs high because of the strong sense of purpose and because the students are researching a topic they chose themselves. When the books are completed, the authors deliver the books to the elementary classroom.

In a similar project, the older students choose an insect or animal as a subject for study. They write a careful account of its actions and behavior over a period of days. Then, using their notes, they write a narrative for young children. These books often become picture books for preschoolers.

What Do Scientists Do?

To encourage interest in science, teachers need to create opportunities for students to be scientists, not just passively learn information that scientists provide. To be a scientist means to plan and work through a research project. Applying scientific inquiry to a problem that needs to be solved helps students understand how concepts are formed. One project that teaches scientific inquiry with a high level of motivation is "Oobleck," designed by teacher Sue Hall. Hall based her unit on a GEMS series book titled *Oobleck*. This project puts into action a quote from *Science for All Americans:* "The validity of scientific claims are settled by referring to observations of phenomena" (Rutherford & Ahlgren, 1990, p. 5). Although Hall taught this unit to fifth-graders, I have also used it successfully with high school students.

The term *Oobleck* comes from the book *Bartholomew and the Oobleck* by Dr. Suess. Younger students usually know the story, but it is a good idea to begin by reading the book aloud regardless of the age of the students. Following the reading, the teacher explains that our space program has sent a probe to another planet and discovered that it was covered with large green oceans of material similar to Oobleck. The space scientists were able to retrieve some Oobleck to bring back to earth for study. Their first job is to describe the properties of Oobleck.

The students work in small groups as a team of scientists. In their journals they explain what a property is. How do they go about determining the properties of an unknown strange substance? At this point, each group receives a container of Oobleck that the teacher has made up ahead of time.

Oobleck

> 4 boxes of cornstarch
> $6\,^3/_4$ cups water
> 15 drops of green food color
>
> Mix the water and food color in a large
> bowl and gradually add the cornstarch.
> from *Oobleck*, LHS GEMS

Each group carries out several experiments to determine the properties. Close observations and detailed notes of results are necessary for accurate data collection. Each group reports its findings to the other groups. Discussion follows and then each property is voted on. If three-quarters of the members of the class agree, the property becomes a Law of Oobleck. Each group then works on writing a description of Oobleck based on its properties.

The next day the student scientists again meet in their small groups and design a spacecraft that will be able to land on the oceans of Oobleck, explore the planet, and return to earth. Each group draws a projected spacecraft design and prepares a report for presenting their design to the rest of the class. As a follow-up activity, Hall has the students describe ways they behaved like scientists during the project. How did they use the inquiry approach, confer with others, and ultimately come to conclusions?

In another example of investigative science, students choose an advertising claim to investigate—for example, how long cereal stays crisp in milk, how easily stains are removed from cloth, how absorbent are paper towels, or how cookies compare in nutritional values. The students work in groups and set up the study. They must control the variables and replicate the study. Each group writes a report of the findings.

Informational Science Writing

Writing to impart information often takes this tack: "Tell me what you know and I (teacher) will tell you if it is enough." There are times when this approach is appropriate, as in a test situation; but for students to learn, a different purpose is needed. We all learn best when we solve problems that are important to us. A good way to have students involved in finding out about a subject is to have them write a script for a television documentary. If a teacher has the resources, actually having the students produce the show is extremely beneficial to the learning process. The students work in groups, choosing a subject that interests them. Or the class as a whole can select topics of interest, and the groups are then arranged according to interest. The teacher shows one or two documentaries and leads a discussion on the type and source of information; the intended audience; and the use of action shots, interviews, and questions. Students are encouraged to use a variety of sources for the information: professional people, laypeople, experiments, and printed material. Because the written work is in the form of a script, students will benefit from seeing copies of other scripts. In producing the show, the students will need music, artwork, and slides. Students will play the parts of experts and others whom they interviewed, although they may have some captured with a video camera. Editing, as in real life, requires a great deal of commitment from the students and is necessary to produce an interesting video. A teacher might be able to arrange with public access to air the shows.

Learning Log Activities

Keeping a notebook or journal will help students accurately describe observations "that carefully distinguish actual observation from ideas and speculation about what was observed, and is understandable weeks or months later" (Rutherford & Ahlgren, 1990, p. 179). Writing observations in a journal increases one's ability to notice details. Teachers can create opportunities by asking students to record sunsets or other natural occurrences for a week to heighten their observational skills.

To encourage students to use their learning logs as a tool for learning, a chemistry teacher had students write everything they knew as a review before a quiz. The entries were used during the review session. The teacher did not read them. The logs might be used in an open-book exam or as an introduction to a homework assignment.

A middle school teacher had students record the weather in their journals to heighten their awareness of the environment. In addition to what they observed, students predicted the temperature, wind, and precipitation for the following day.

When students are required to use the journal as a method of keeping track of observations, they begin to be more aware of the world around them. This is helpful not only in science but in other subjects as well. The same assignment can be used for a science class and an English class, but for different purposes.

One example is having students record everything they see, hear, feel, and smell from the same vantage point for one week. They are to make the observations twice a day if possible, but at least once a day. Their own yard is a convenient and adequate place for the observations which are written in their journals. For a science class, the notes provide data for an ecology unit or a unit on habitat

---

FIGURE 7-1   Awareness Worksheet

1. Using all of your senses, notice the wind. In what ways are you aware of the wind? Be specific with details and observations. What direction is the wind coming from?

2. Close your eyes and concentrate on everything you can hear. At first you will hear the loudest, most obvious noises. Relax and keep listening—the softer background noises will become clearer.

3. How many different kinds of trees can you see? Either name them (e.g., an oak tree) or describe them in detail: texture and color of the bark; shape of the overall tree; approximate height, shape, and size of the leaves.

4. Take a deep breath and concentrate on all that you can smell.

5. Closely examine one square foot of ground. Write down everything you see. Describe the blades of grass, soil, insects, worms, flowering plants. Look for the smallest detail.

6. What do you think the temperature is? Will it rain today? What is the wind velocity?

---

or the weather. Students are encouraged to look for connections and patterns in their observations. For English, the same notes provide a setting for a narrative or an idea for a story line. The wealth of details the data provide helps a reader see what the writer saw. To help guide their observations, the worksheet in Figure 7–1 might be helpful, at least to get them started.

A similar, but more comprehensive, activity is one on signs of a seasonal change. Students keep a journal recording their observations on, for example, every sign of spring they can observe. The observations are not limited to nature but can include every type of sign possible—human behavior, store sales, music, food. Class discussions based on their journals, newspaper articles, folklore, common knowledge, and weather forecasts occur while students continue observing signs. As a final project, students write a paper based on their journals.

Writing in Health Class

Because of the importance of health education in their lives, it is vital that students take an active part in their learning in this area. We want students to take responsibility for gathering information and understanding the concepts of good health. A few examples of how writing can help students and teachers reach those goals are described here.

Rather than write a report on a particular aspect of health, students benefit more from composing a pamphlet that can be used to provide information to others. The pamphlets available in all doctors' offices are a good starting place. Usually, these pamphlets are written for adults and deal with a particular disease or condition. Students should plan their pamphlets for an audience of peers or younger children. Working in pairs, students choose a topic that interests them. Food disorders, safety in sports, exercise, immunizations, common diseases, prevention, treating bruises, and broken bones are a few possible examples. Illustrations lend interest to the pamphlets, and layout is important. If the students have access to software programs, the results can be quite professional looking; in any case, students learn a great deal throughout the project. If appropriate, the pamphlets can be copied and shared with people outside the classroom.

Gathering data on the nutritional value of student lunches is both informative and interesting to secondary students. The project works best if done in groups of about six students. One group could collect data on the hot lunch program, another on a sampling of lunches brought from home, another on lunches purchased at fast food places. Students should also check on which foods are actually eaten and which are tossed. This information can be collected through surveys, observation, and interviews. Once the foods are identified, the students figure out the nutritional value from appropriate sources. Finally, each group writes up a report that is shared with other class members and perhaps as a feature article in the school newspaper.

An interesting project for health class is to have students study old-time remedies for common diseases and discover whether this folklore has any validity. First, students discuss remedies they have heard of, perhaps from family members, or have read about. Older recipe books are a good source of information, as are reference books on medical history. A recipe book published in the 1950s contains many suggestions for using herbs for medicinal purposes: Anise seed aids digestion and "disturbances by overeating," chamomile tea soothes children with colic (like Peter Rabbit), tea made from thyme quiets nightmares (examples taken from the *Favorite Recipe Cook Book*, Saints Peter & Paul's Ukrainian Catholic Church, Chisholm, Minnesota, published in 1958). In this book and elsewhere are many more suggestions for easing headaches, hiccoughs, coughs, and other ailments. After students collect the folklore remedies, they investigate the possible validity of the cures by more reading and by interviewing health care workers. Working in groups, they write a report on their findings that is compiled into a class book.

Summary

Writing in math and science helps students become actively involved in their own learning. Students learn to be creative and responsive to the physical world. Through writing, they learn to explain difficulties they are having, thus making it easier for teachers to address problems. Journals help students and teachers communicate, and writing technical language in their own words aids in understanding. Working in groups as real scientists do is helpful in creative thinking and problem solving. At every level of learning, writing is important to comprehending and remembering.

Discussion Questions

1. Write your own math history, and compare it with those of others in your group. How does the way you view math relate to your early learning experiences?
2. Discuss how the new NCTM standards would change the math teaching in the high school you attended.
3. What do you see as the most difficult aspect of teaching science or math?
4. Discuss how you could teach math and/or science to adapt to a variety of learning styles.
5. How does writing help you to learn concepts in your college classes?

Suggested Activities

1. Devise a math activity that would help secondary students understand terminology.
2. Most of the writing examples in this chapter are considered level 1. Describe two or three level 2 writing activities and explain what purpose they would serve in learning math or science.
3. Plan an activity for a physics class that incorporates group discussion and writing.
4. Revise a typical chemistry lab report that requires short answers so that thoughtful explanations are called for.
5. Construct a math exam that reflects the new NCTM standards.
6. As a group activity, devise a hands-on science activity that requires group work, similar to the Oobleck experiment.

References

Casteel, Carolyn P., & Bess A. Isom. "Reciprocal Process in Science and Literacy Learning." *The Reading Teacher, 47,* 1994, pp. 538–545.

Countryman, Joan. "Writing to Learn Mathematics." *Teaching K–8.* January 1993, pp. 51–53.

Fortescue, Chelsea M. "Using Oral and Written Language to Increase Understanding of Math Concepts." *Language Arts, 71,* December 1994, pp. 576–580.

Gaskins, Irene W., et al. "Classroom Talk about Text: Learning in Science Class." *Journal of Reading, 37,* 1994, pp. 558–565.

Johnson, Patricia. "Writing to Learn Science." In Anne Ruggles Gere, ed., *Roots in the Sawdust* (pp. 92–103). Urbana, IL: National Council of Teachers of English, 1985.

Jones, M. Gail. "Performance-based Assessment in Middle School Science." *Middle School Journal,* March 1994, pp. 35–38.

Kenyon, Russel W. "Using Writing in Mathematics." In Dale Worsley & Bernadette Mayer, *The Art of Science Writing* (pp. 199–204). New York: Teachers & Writers Collaborative, 1989.

Maxwell, Rhoda, & Stephen Judy. "Science Writing in the English Classroom." *English Journal,* April 1978, pp. 78–81.

Miller, Diane L. "Making the Connection with

Language." *Arithmetic Teacher*, February 1993, pp. 311–316.

Mulholland, Vivienne. "Mathematics across the Curriculum." *Early Child Development and Care, 82*, 1992, pp. 37–47.

Rutherford, F. James, & Andrew Ahlgren. *Science for All Americans*. New York: Oxford University Press, 1990.

Salem, Judith. "Using Writing in Teaching Mathematics." In Mary Barr, Pat D'Arcy, & Mary Healy, eds., *What's Going On?* (pp. 123–134). Montclair, NJ: Boynton/Cook, 1982.

Saul, Wendy, & Sybille A. Jagusch, eds. *Vital Connections*. Portsmouth, NH: Heinemann, 1991.

Scarnati, James T. "Interview with a Wild Animal: Integrating Science and Language Arts." *Middle School Journal*, March 1994, pp. 3–6.

Schmidt, Don. "Writing in Math Class." In Anne Ruggles Gere, ed., *Roots in the Sawdust* (pp. 104–116). Urbana, IL: National Council of Teachers of English, 1985.

Wadlington, Elizabeth, Joe Bitner, Elizabeth Par-

tridge, & Sue Austin. "Writing–Mathematics Connection." *Arithmetic Teacher*, December 1992, pp. 207–209.

Wagler, Mark. "What's a Mathematician?" *It Figures!* Madison Metropolitan School District, May 1993, pp. 86–92.

Walpole, Pam. "Yes, Writing in Math." *Plain Talk*, Virginia Department of Education, Spring 1987, pp. 51–59.

Watts, Sue. "Science: Writing and Understanding—Writing and Learning." In Nancy Martin, ed., *Writing Across the Curriculum* (pp. 114–120). Montclair, NJ: Boynton/Cook, 1984.

Wood, Karen D. "Fostering Collaborative Reading and Writing Experiences in Mathematics." *Journal of Reading, 36*(2), October 1992, pp. 96–103.

Worsley, Dale, & Bernadette Mayer. *The Art of Science Writing*. New York: Teachers & Writers Collaborative, 1989.

8

WRITING IN SOCIAL STUDIES

Writing not only deepens understanding and aids retention, but also unifies the social studies to enhance students' sense of citizenship and civic responsibility.
—*HILARY TAYLOR HOLBROOK 1988, P. 216*

Prereading Questions

1. What are the major roles of writing in social studies?
2. What are the content areas of social studies? How might writing help students learn the content of each area?
3. Recently the social studies curriculum has gone through major changes. How has the teaching of social studies changed over the past ten years?
4. How can level 1 or informal writing be utilized in social studies?
5. What was your favorite social studies activity or unit when you were in middle school and high school? What did you like about it?

Introduction

Writing requires that students become active participants in their learning and, consequently, take an in-depth approach to social studies. In a booklet outlining the new directions in social studies, Frederick Risinger states, "While writing is important throughout the curriculum, nowhere is the impact greater than in social studies. The very nature of the subject requires the thoughtful deliberation inherent in conceptualizing a topic and then explaining it in writing" (Risinger, 1992, p. 16). Rather than passively learning facts, writing helps students make comparisons, differentiate between fact and opinion, understand relationships among events, people, and land, and describe cause and effect. "Writing provides the best vehicle for students to demonstrate these skills, which are most often associated with critical thinking" (Risinger, 1992, p. 16). Social studies requires critical thinking because of the difficult concepts necessary to learning citizenship and civic responsibility.

A teacher, Kim O'Day, makes a strong case for the importance of writing in social studies. She states that "geographers, psychologists, and other specialists in social studies must constantly update their knowledge. Students face the same challenge" (O'Day, 1994, p. 39). Writing is an important part of social scientists' work: "historians report; geographers and anthropologists record observations; and psychologists develop statements or analyses based upon data they have logged" (p. 39). In a classroom, through reading and writing, students learn to recognize author bias, which is essential to understanding prejudice and opinion. Students' understanding of history increases when they explore attitudes and feelings in historical events. "Writing, whether it is critical, narrative, or interpretive, propels them into also analyzing the event" (p. 39). Becoming active learners through writing, thinking, and analyzing helps students gain deeper understandings of people the world over.

Types of Writing

Writing is integral in the units and themes taught in social science courses and, depending on the purpose of the writing, may be creative, informal, involved, short, long, individual, or group work. Incorporating writing activities within the social studies curriculum helps students to organize the information better and make connections with what they already know (Holbrook, 1988, p. 216). Although some teachers limit writing in social studies to report writing, many types of writing are appropriate and add to students' learning social studies content: informative, poetic, personal, formal, descriptive, and fictional. The importance of writing in social studies cannot be overstated. Students who participate in a writing-to-learn approach in the classroom are likely to learn more content, understand it better, and retain it longer (Myers, 1984).

The writing-to-learn approach includes all three levels of writing, as well as a variety of types of writing. Through using level 1 writing, students have opportunities "to formulate the course material into their own language and to learn that material" (Lehning, 1993, p. 342). This informal style of writing provides a starting point for class discussions. "Words make thought concrete and real, shaping experience" (Lehning, 1993, p. 340). By devoting more time to informal writing and less time to formal, teachers provide opportunities for their students to put their thoughts into words and therefore gain control over the knowledge. Writing as a mode of learning becomes a reality in classes where students can use writing to express thoughts, to remember what they learn, discover what they need to find out, organize and connect what they are learning.

Writing is a resource for learning because it "provides strategies for expressing and then examining thoughts" (Winchell & Elder, 1994, p. 273). Also, writing "allows the writer to organize complex bodies of information," and helps make course "content more completely understood and remembered" (p. 273). Social science specialists value an inquiry approach to teaching and learning; such an approach requires original sources, interviews, firsthand experiences, and observation (Sturtevant, 1994, p. 96). Making sense of such diverse sources of knowledge, and then creating connections and meaning, requires a variety of writing purposes and forms. As an example, Sturtevant suggests that a unit of study on the Vietnam War could include a multiplicity of original sources: letters, interviews, museums, related literature, and news accounts (p. 96).

Writing Activities

The remainder of this chapter describes successful writing activities from history, geography, and social studies classes.

Writing Microthemes

Stephen Kneeshaw, a history professor, has devised a short writing activity that provides frequent opportunities for students to respond to topics, readings, and discussion questions. The microthemes are written on 5 x 8 cards and can be handwritten or typed. They might be assigned to draw together ideas from a lecture or readings, and thus be a starting point for a following discussion period. Kneeshaw uses a variety of approaches in designing the microthemes, which might include an interpretation of a historic event, an explanation of a topic such as the balance of power in the U.S. Constitution; an assignment to compare, contrast, and analyze; an analysis of course materials; or summaries of outside readings (Kneeshaw, 1992, p. 177). One advantage of the microthemes is that they are fairly easy and quick to evaluate because of the length and the focus on content. Students also like them because they are limited in length and helpful when studying. Students "learn that good writing does not demand length but instead relies on careful thought and precise word selection" (p. 178).

Writing Travel Brochures

When studying countries, writing a brochure has several advantages over the standard report. Because the sense of audience is strong after a discussion about who reads brochures and why they are written, students are more likely to use pertinent information and less likely to copy facts mindlessly from an encyclopedia. Each piece of information must focus on the thesis of the brochure. To write an interesting brochure, students need to read widely about the country before deciding on the focus of the brochure. Possibilities include the historical approach, the natural beauty, or the people. As with all report writing, students should jot down the questions the brochure will answer before digging into resource material. If students have access to a computer layout program, the brochure can look professional, which adds to the sense of accomplishment. For students who enjoy art, the brochure provides opportunities to use their artistic abilities. This idea can be linked to literature by having students write a brochure on an imaginary country found in fiction; examples from science fiction are especially intriguing.

Brochures about Constitutional Amendments

Brad Matott, a social studies teacher, used the brochure idea when his students studied countries. The students enjoyed the creative experience and learned much about the countries as well. For these reasons, Matott decided to use the brochure activity when his eighth-graders studied constitutional amendments. His purpose was to have students show what they had learned from their studies in ways other than by taking traditional tests. Students worked in groups of two or three, with each group responsible for creating a brochure that advertised one of the amendments. The brochures were then shared with the whole class. The experience was rewarding because students learned about the amendments in a way that will stay with them for a long time. An example by students Jessa Olien and Mary Parrot is shown in Figure 8–1(a) and 8–1(b).

Writing a Recruiting Campaign

Having students act as recruiting agents for the thirteen original American colonies is an excellent way of involving them in learning American history (Evans, 1993). Evans has each student select the name of one colony from a hat and then research that colony. Students are encouraged to use a variety of resources: books, brochures, films, slides, and filmstrips. After completing the research, the students write a report in a level 2 format and prepare to share their material with the class. They must use "some artistic means of demonstration, such as signs or posters" in the presentation (Evans, 1993, p. 337). Some students dress in Colonial fashion; others prepare appropriate food or illustrate products. They emphasize the benefits of living in their particular colony, which might include farming opportunities, religious tolerance, or democratic rule.

A similar way to involve students in their learning was designed by Jim Jeffries, a high school history and English teacher, for his tenth-grade history class. While studying the early development of the American colonies, students were to choose one colony and describe its ethnic, political, and social attributes from the point of view of one person. The report was a personification of the time period in a specific region. To begin, Jeffries gave each student a general outline. An example of the general outline by a student is shown in Figure 8–2. Figure 8–3 shows the first few paragraphs of the student's paper, illustrating his first draft and his subsequent revisions. These same paragraphs from his final paper are in Figure 8–4. This example of Gordon's paper illustrates how the writing process is carried through to a level 3 paper.

FIGURE 8-1(a)   Cover of Brochure

FIGURE 8-1(b)   Inside the Brochure

lately my son has been
looking thinner
because the soldiers stole
his dinner
At night they take his bed
where he must rest his head
The boy's name is Rick
I think he's getting sick!
I tell them to leave-
for winning the war is their
goal to achive.
They say that next Sunday
night
They will go and win that
fight.

A woman remembers-
"When I was in my house
one day a soldier came,
Knocked on the door
and told me he now
lived with me. I had
3 children and little
money. He ate our
food, was rude and
robbed us of our few
belongings. My youngest
son was starved

<u>KEEP SOLDIERS OUT</u>!

FIGURE 8-2   Persona

Name: Aaron Lopez
Resident: Newport, Rhode Island
Age: 39
Family History: Originally from Portugal, left because of the Inquisition. One
   brother immigrated with me, Ben.
Occupation: Merchant, slave trader, whaler near Falkland, island shipper
Political Beliefs: Aristocrat
Personal History: Founded Touro Synagogue, very wealthy, wife named
   Sara with two kids.

Writing That Links Social Studies and Journalism

Linking social studies with journalism improves students' role in citizenship education. Social studies teachers can work cooperatively with journalism teachers
to provide opportunities for students to gain experiences in writing, reporting,

FIGURE 8-3   Aaron Lopez

Aaron Lopez

My name is Aaron Lopez. My life story is one from rags to riches. I started out in a small town [*Portuguese*] living in poverty, to a luxurious life in the new world called America. I will tell my story from birth in Combria to the present day in 1770.

On March 29, 1732 my parents ~~Fernando~~ [*Carlos*] and ~~Anna~~ [*Juanita*] Lopez were blessed with their first child, me. I grew up [*on a poor*] ~~very poverty stricken~~ farm in rural Combria. [*My family was not the only family who were poor*] ~~along with many other people~~ in this small town. My family had a ~~very~~ hard time surviving in this Christian community [*because*] We were a Jewish family. ~~was under~~ [*living secret lives as Christians*] ~~the assumption of all the towne people~~ being Christian just like them. ~~If any one~~ [*Mr. I*] ~~body~~ knew we were Jewish we would be burned at the stake or beheaded. The Inquisition in Portugal was very tough on my family forcing us to ~~get out of~~ [*leave*] Portugal. Our family was ~~planing~~ [*planning*] to move to the colonies when my mother and father fell ill [*of*] ~~to~~ a deadly fever. My brother [*Benjamin then left*] and I were the only members of my family to move to the colonies.

I arrived in America on March 29, 1750, my twentieth birthday ~~in Boston Massachusetts~~ [*Boston MA. This was*]. My trip to the colonies was a ~~very~~ long and gruesome ~~ride~~ [*Journey*]. ~~Only 152 arrived alive, our ship carried 300 people~~ [*people Survives our ship*] [*Since began our trek*]. My brother and I were extremely lucky. I did not want to go through the secret life of a Jew in this new land, so I decided to live openly. I soon ~~~~ [*heard the*] of colony named Rhode Island. This colony gave religious tolerance to all people. I moved there immediately. My new home was Newport, Rhode Island. Not ~~everybody~~ [*everyone*] in this Colony ~~got~~ [*lived in harmony however kept*] ~~along together, but if you stuck~~ to your ~~own~~ [*self*] business people usually left you alone. I soon got my first job. Hired by a wealthy merchant to run his store. We sold everything. I did not stay there long because I knew how much money he ~~made there and~~ [*was making. I knew I could be a success.*] soon started my own business. My business flourished for we [*S I*] were the only merchants in the new a rapidly growing town [*of Newport*]. I ~~got~~ the majority of ~~the~~ [*the towns*] business because I lowered my prices drastically and did not tax anything. [*earned*] I knew the law had taxes on ~~a lot of~~ [*many the*] goods but I ignored them. I suppose I could have been in ~~big~~ [*serious*] trouble with the Crown, but the ~~~~ [*tax*] laws were not enforced here.

[*Only 152 people Survived out of 300 the Trip*]

and researching. Additionally, social studies teachers can incorporate newspaper activities into the classroom. Suggestions from several teachers illustrate this combination:

1. *Futuristic writing:* Working in groups, students select five items from a current newspaper; these can be a combination of feature stories, reports, news, and in-depth investigations. Using the same format, they rewrite the story as it might appear one hundred years from now, or write it as a follow-up to an event that

FIGURE 8–4 Final Paper, Aaron Lopez

Aaron Gordon

Grade 10

My name is Aaron Lopez. My life story is one from rags to riches. I started out in a small Portuguese town living in poverty, to a luxurious life in the New World called America. I will tell my story from birth in Combria to the present day in 1770.

On March 29, 1732, my parents, Carlos and Juanita Lopez, were blessed with their first child, me. I grew up on a very poor farm in rural Combria. My family was not the only family who were poor in this small town. My family had a hard time surviving in this Christian community. We were a Jewish family living secret lives as Christains just like them. If anyone knew we were Jewish we would be burned at the stake or beheaded. The Inquisition in Portugal was very tough on my family, forcing us to leave Portugal. Our family was planning to move to the colonies when my mother and father fell ill of a deadly fever. My brother Benjamin and I were then the only members of my family left to move to the colonies.

I arrived in Boston, Massachusetts, America, on March 29, 1750. This was my twentieth birthday. My trip to the colonies was a long and gruesome journey. Only 152 people out of 300 survived the trip. My brother and I were extremely lucky. I did not want to go through the secret life of a Jew in this new land, so I decided to live openly. I soon heard of the colony named Rhode Island. This colony gave religious tolerance to all people. I moved there immediately. My new home was Newport, Rhode Island. Not everyone in this colony lived in

---

FIGURE 8-4 *Continued*

harmony; however, if you kept to yourself people usually left
you alone. I soon got my first job, hired by a wealthy merchant to run his store. We sold everything. I did not stay
there long; I knew how much money he was making. Soon I
started my own business. I knew I could become a success.
My business flourished, for we were the only merchants in the
new and rapidly growing town of Newport. I earned the majority
of the town's business because I lowered my prices drastically
and did not tax anything. I knew the law had taxes on many of
the goods, but I ignored them. I suppose I could have been in
serious trouble with the Crown, but the tax laws were not
enforced here.

---

happened now. Examples could include earthquakes, wars, economic situations, governments in various countries, or world relations. Having students begin with newspaper articles helps focus their writing and makes it more realistic. The reports are collected in a mock newspaper and posted in the classroom. Depending on how many classes a teacher has, the wide variety of approaches makes interesting reading.

2. *Editorial writing:* When studying the American Revolution, students write three one-page editorials from three different perspectives. The first is that of a pro-revolutionary colonial paper, the second that of a Colonial loyalist. The third perspective should reflect the French government's decision to join the Americans in their fight for liberty. By writing thoughtful editorials from three different points of view, students gain a better understanding of the issues (Risinger, 1992, p. 17).

3. *Comparison writing:* Compare news coverage across countries or cities by having students read newspapers from different locations. Newspapers from local libraries are a good source. Each student or group reads the same news story and compares the coverage. The comparison can cover the headline, placement, details, length, position in the paper, and content of material. The story should be followed for several days. Then the students write a paper reporting their findings. Students compare their results and, through discussion, make observations about the reasons for differences in coverage.

4. *Additional activities for linking newspapers and social studies:* Lynn Rhoades has developed many ideas using the daily newspaper to teach cognitive skill development. A selected few are included here. She has worded them as an assignment directed to the students.

- Find national or international news stories that might affect you or your community. Explain in writing how the situation could affect your area.
- Describe which problems discussed in the newspaper are caused by geographical features or location.
- Plan an imaginary interview with a government official. Write the interview questions.
- Follow the president for a week by reading all the newspaper items you can find about him. Write a summary of his weekly activities and your evaluation of them.
- Write a plan for a goodwill trip the president will make. Which countries should he visit and why? Which leaders should he meet with and why? What points of U.S. policy need to be discussed on this trip?

Writing That Examines Preconceived Ideas

Activities designed to help students examine their beliefs and biases teach them to rethink hasty judgments. "Students have many inaccurate perceptions of the world because they are not familiar with the information, are inundated with media stereotypes or have limited opportunities to think for themselves" (Richburg, Nelson, & Reid, 1994, p. 66). A way of helping students to think about their judgments is to design questions where the "obvious" answer is incorrect because students have inaccurate or incomplete information. For example, who is held in the highest esteem of all their great historic figures by the French people? One might suggest Napoleon or DeGaulle or Joan of Arc, but recent surveys show it is Louis Pasteur. For Germans, the person held in the highest esteem is not Bismarck, but Dietrich Bonhöfer (p. 66). Using many examples from social studies will help students learn to reexamine their knowledge. Richburg, Nelson, and Reid provide several questions to heighten student awareness (p. 66). The following three are examples:

1. Which two nations produce more oil than any other in the world—Saudi Arabia, Kuwait, Venezuela, the United States, or the former Soviet Union? (The correct answer is the United States and the former Soviet Union)
2. Which city has the highest yearly average snowfall—Minneapolis, Flagstaff, or Denver? (Flagstaff)
3. Which of these nations has the highest infant and child mortality rates—Japan, Sweden, Switzerland, the United States, Iceland, or Syria? (the United States)

"Stereotypes of groups of people are perhaps the most powerful opportunities for challenge as students confront issues related to age, ethnicity, gender, or disability" (Richburg et al., 1994, p. 67). Actions and beliefs based on misinformation can lead to serious consequences. As teachers, we need to help students face their misconceptions, and questions such as these make them confront their faulty conclusions.

In a related activity, Lynn Burlbaw describes a lesson that demonstrates the problems with making decisions based on incomplete evidence:

> Teachers must be aware that generalizations can be difficult to teach and, unless carefully taught, can result in stereotyping as students over-apply what they know to situations for which they have incomplete or insufficient information. (Burlbaw, 1994, p. 110)

Her lesson plan involves four diagrams, each containing different types and amounts of information on the possible town site at the intersection of a river and a town. Figure 1 shows the coastline, Figure 2 the water depth, Figure 3 the land topography, and Figure 4 the vegetation. Burlbaw begins by explaining the usefulness of generalizations in making decisions. The diagrams are on transparencies and are shown in order to the students. With only the information from Figure 1, the discussion leads students to suggest that any location is appropriate. With the knowledge present in Figure 2 showing the water depth, students might decide that the town site would be best by the deeper water level for a port. Figure 3 shows that because of a high cliff, loading and unloading ships would be too difficult. With the fourth transparency laid over the other three, the students can see the best site for the town because they now have access to more information. The activity shows graphically the importance of having as complete information as possible before making a decision.

Writing Reports

Report writing involves gathering information from a variety of sources. Social studies reports, in particular, need resources beyond traditional textbooks. To develop critical thinking skills, students must recognize that history accounts depend on who is telling the story. The same is true in current affairs. Issues have many sides, and a clear right–wrong dichotomy rarely exists. Newspapers, journals, popular magazines, films, radio and television, interviews, personal observations and experiences are all resources for writing reports. When possible, students should use primary sources such as actual letters, diaries, and journals written by people in the historical time period. In writing a report, students begin searching for material, analyzing information, and then deciding what additional information is needed. The final report should reflect what they discovered and the conclusions they have reached. Report-writing assignments with an added dimension of creativity are more interesting for students; consequently, their writing has more depth and detail.

Students may have difficulty finding appropriate material, focusing on main points, and organizing their writing. One way to help students manage the material and not lose sight of their goal of writing a comprehensive report is to have them list the attributes that support a concept. Dimmitt and Van Cleaf (1992) provide an example of students studying Jacksonian democracy who listed attributes of Jackson:

> Jackson had the support of the common person.
>
> He was a popular hero.
>
> He believed in democracy.
>
> He told Congress and the Supreme Court what he thought was best for the country.
>
> He did not trust rule by the elite. (p. 383)

Beginning with the list they drew up, students could then find evidence supporting each attribute, which would focus their informational gathering and provide structure for the organization of their final report.

Writing Scripts

First in a large group and then in smaller groups, students discuss current issues that are important to them. Working in a small group, students write a script for a television documentary on one of the social problems they discussed. Each group must study the background material to make the documentary authentic. If possible, they include interviews just as special news programs do. Each group's show is videotaped, and then each is shown to the whole class. Discussion follows about how fair and unbiased the script was toward all involved parties.

Examining Propaganda

Cynthia Sunal and Mary Haas (1994) designed a lesson plan based on the government's efforts during World War I to influence women to take part in the war effort. The resources used in the lesson are the posters designed by the government. Working in small groups, the students analyzed the posters; they were guided by questions provided by the teachers. For example:

1. Which posters do you think were most effective in getting the desired responses from women? Why?
2. Which poster asked women potentially to sacrifice the most?
3. Judging from the suggestions on the posters, what behaviors could the greatest number of American women perform that would help the war effort?

After a class discussion on their findings, the teachers ask the students what propaganda techniques were used. Do they think the same techniques would work today?

A related activity could be about the government's efforts to have women leave the labor force after World War II and return to the home. The resources are not as clearly defined as the posters but are available in women's and news magazines published at the time. Students could identify the techniques used by collecting data on the topics covered in the publications. By examining census data on women in the labor force, they could see how effective the campaign was.

Additional questions to investigate along the same lines are what are the current social pressures on women? On men? Where are the social pressures evident? What media are used? What propaganda, if any, is used today?

Writing Based on Biographies

By reading biographies, students learn to assess and understand events related to a person in a particular time period. Many writing assignments can be based on the biographies, reflecting all three levels of writing and different forms of writing. Students can write postcards as the central character in the book might have done. This encourages them to understand the "person's unique perspective" (Miller, Clegg, & Vanderhoof, 1992, p. 134). The intended recipient might be a contemporary of the person or someone in another historical time period. The postcard should reflect "the appropriate voice, style, or register that the subject would likely have used to write to a particular person" (p. 135).

Pat Stellick has her tenth-grade students write an essay based on biographical material. Her assignment reads as follows:

> In "Open Letter to a Young Negro," "Hilter's Games Tarnished Gold," and *The Jesse Owens Story* video, we were given a variety of views of Jesse Owens. By referring to specific examples from our biographical selections (try to use all three sources), explain in an essay what you think are the most outstanding characteristics of Jesse Owens.

An example of this assignment by Laura Maar, one of Stellick's students, is in Figure 8–5(a) and (b).

Writing Fiction

Having students write fiction based on historical or contemporary events encourages them to investigate beyond the typical text material. Jack McLeod, a middle school teacher, designed the following writing assignment to help stimulate creativity and interest for his students:

> You are a CIA agent. You have spent the past year living in secrecy among the people of Iraq. After risking your life covertly obtaining information, you are now about to send a letter to the president of the United States. You have reached some conclusions regarding relations between Iraq and the United States for the next ten years. In a top secret

FIGURE 8-5 (a)   Drafts and Revisions

Jesse Owens was an outstanding man who cared about the well being of others. Jesse would give money to his friends if they needed help, even if he did not have enough money for himself. He always wanted to help people that *who* were in need and he never looked down on people because their skin was a different color.

For example, in the article "Hitler's Games Tarnished Gold" we read about the time during the 1936 Summer Olympics when Jesse had the chance to run in the 4x~~400~~ *100 meter* relay. By running on the relay team Jesse could possibly win a fourth gold medal. At first he refused because he said that the Jewish athletes Stoller and Glickman worked hard to get to the Olympics and that they deserved to run in the relay. When Jesse objected to running his assistant coach said, "do as you're told." Jesse didn't want to cause trouble, so he ran in the relay. *give a transition* ~~While watching the movie~~ *The Jesse Owens Story*, we also saw an example of Jesse *where a not wanting to cause trouble.* ~~following his orders.~~ On the way to a track meet Jesse and his fellow black teammates stopped at a restaurant to eat. One of Jesse's friends started to get mad when he found out that they *couldn't eat in the restaurant but* had to go outside to eat their food. He started saying how it wasn't fair that they had to eat outside just because they were black. Jesse wanted to just take their food and leave so they wouldn't cause a scene.

Jesse ~~also~~ *obviously* knew what it was like when people judged him by the color of his skin. In "Open Letter to a Young Negro" we're told about the time when Jesse met Luz Long, Germany's best Aryan broad jumper. When Jesse met his rival, he didn't judge Luz for what he was on the outside. Instead Jesse looked past his skin color to what was within. Luz did the same thing for Jesse.

Jesse Owens was an outstanding person both physically and morally. He would always think about other people and how they felt. Jesse will always be remembered for being a star athlete, but people will never forget all of the good things that he did.

letter to the president, present your plan and convince the president that this is the course he and the United States should follow. (McLeod, 1992, p. 398)

This assignment requires current resources and leads students to newspapers and articles. The sense of the spy and top secret information appeals to middle school students (p. 398).

Experiencing the Legal System

Karen Hicks and Jordan Austin have designed a unit that involves the community, problem solving, writing, and oral skills. To begin they asked students "to clip articles from newspapers that showed problems in the community or the

FIGURE 8-5(b)   Jesse Owens, Final Copy

Jesse Owens was an outstanding man who cared about the well being of others. Jesse would give money to his friends if they needed help, even if he did not have enough money for himself. He always wanted to help people who were in need, and he never looked down on people because their skin was a different color.

For example, in the article "Hitler's Games Tarnished Gold" we read about the time during the 1936 Summer Olympics when Jesse had the chance to run in the 4x100 meter relay. By running on the relay team Jesse could possibly win a fourth gold medal. At first he refused because he said that the Jewish athletes Stoller and Glickman worked hard to get to the Olympics and that they deserved to run in the relay. When Jesse objected to running his assistant coach said, "Do as you're told." Jesse didn't want to cause trouble, so he ran in the relay.

In the movie *The Jesse Owens Story,* we also saw an example where Jesse did not want to cause trouble. On the way to a track meet Jesse and his fellow black teammates stopped at a restaurant to eat. One of Jesse's friends started to get mad when he found out that they couldn't eat in the restaurant, but had to go outside to eat their food. He started saying how it wasn't fair that they had to eat outside just because they were black. Jesse wanted to just take their food and leave so they wouldn't cause a scene.

Jesse obviously knew what it was like when people judged him by the color of his skin. In "Open Letter to a Young Negro" we're told about the time when Jesse met Luz Long, Germany's best Aryan broad jumper. When Jesse met his rival, he didn't judge Luz for what he was on the outside. Instead, Jesse looked past his skin color to what was within. Luz did the same thing for Jesse and they soon became good friends.

Jesse Owens was an outstanding person both physically and morally. He would always think about other people and how they felt. Jesse will always be remembered for being a star athlete, but people will never forget all of the good things that he did for others.

world to help make them aware of similarities among personal problems, community problems, and world problems" (p. 39). Discussions about the various problems centered on how these problems were or were not solved. The next step in the unit was to study the legal system as it represents institutionalized problem solving. Local law enforcement officers were invited to class to talk about statutes of criminal behavior, their definitions, and their consequences. To make the information more interesting, the students looked at well-known fairy stories for examples of criminal behavior and supported their opinion with facts from the stories. Folktales could be used, or any fictional story. With help from the local law enforcement agency, students can learn what the legal issues are and what consequences can result. For instance, students would need to know the meanings of terms like *criminal mischief, aggravated robbery, criminal impersonation, harassment, fraud, felony,* and *manslaughter.* After comparing stories and engaging in lengthy discussion, each class decides on what story to use as the basis for their mock trial so that students can experience the judicial system at work.

Austin contacted attorneys and a judge to set up the learning experience. In Austin's unit, the lawyers and judges actually took part in the mock trial; if that is not possible to arrange, students can play these parts, but they would have to work closely with professionals so that the trial is authentic. Prior to the trial, the students chose the parts they wanted to play. They used Jon Scieszka's *The True Story of the Three Little Pigs* to understand how any situation depends on point of view.

The class learned and discussed the power of language in influencing our judgment. The power of oral and written language was emphasized throughout the mock trial. The students studied their state's criminal statutes and became familiar with relevant terminology.

To represent the character they chose to play, students dressed in costume, created photo albums of drawings of their character's home and life, and wrote journal entries in the persona of their character. Austin's students chose "Hansel and Gretel." On the day of the trial, law enforcement officers arrested the stepmother and the old woman in the forest on charges of attempted murder and child abuse. Their Miranda rights were read to them, and they were taken to the jail to await trial, which began immediately.

The defense lawyer painted a picture of the old woman as a lonely widow, a bit eccentric; the prosecuting attorney described her as a witch. He brought in two expert witnesses, Brother Grimm and Bruno Bettleheim, to prove his point. Discussion arose about the reliability of the two witnesses. The importance and power of language became more obvious. The outcome of this trial was that the two were found guilty, but the learning that occurred was the more important outcome.

The students learned the importance of differentiating fact from opinion, hearsay, and circumstantial evidence. As a result of the mock trial, Austin's students became "more specific in their wording, careful in their judgments, aware of bias and prejudice" (p. 42). The collaboration between the school and community in this project is an important model for teaching units.

Summary

Writing is an important part of social scientists' work and, therefore, is important for students learning social studies. Writing helps students to make comparisons, differentiate between facts and opinions, understand relationships, and describe cause and effect. By using a wide variety of writing types such as informative, poetic, fictional, and personal, students can begin to analyze historical events and judge the many sides of current situations. Writing helps students become informed citizens.

Discussion Questions

1. One of the goals in social studies is to help students develop good citizenship. What does being a good citizen mean to you?
2. How can we make the world a better place?
3. Students, especially in junior high or middle school, are often concerned if something is fair or not. How does one decide if something is fair? Define *justice* and *equality*. How can teachers make such abstract words meaningful to students?
4. Propaganda is widely used to influence people's behavior. Discuss when and how it is used. Do you believe it is ever appropriate? Never? Always?
5. What are the distinctions between facts and knowledge?

Suggested Activities

1. Select an issue that is personally important to you. Write as many viewpoints as possible concerning the issue. Describe ways that you could help students recognize the complexity of an issue.
2. How do values and behaviors influence each other? Design a lesson for middle school students helping them to identify their values. How would you change the lesson for high school students?
3. Watch the evening news on the major networks for several days. Compare and analyze the news presentations. What conclusions can you draw about the networks' political stance and biases? How can you use this information in developing lesson plans for future students?
4. Watch and analyze TV commercials over a period of a week. What conclusions can you draw about U.S. society? What stereotypes are presented? In particular, look at the way minorities, women, teenagers, and older people are portrayed. Design a lesson based on your findings.
5. Design a unit that involves the community as a resource.

References

Burlbaw, Lynn Matthew. "Applying Generalizations in Middle School Geography Classes." *The Social Studies*, May–June 1994, pp. 110–113.

Dimmitt, Jean Pollard, & David W. Van Cleaf. "Integrating Writing and Social Studies: Alternatives to the Formal Research Paper." *Social Education*, 56(7), 1992, pp. 382–383.

Evans, Michael C. "Recruiting American Colonists among Eighteenth-Century Europeans: A Social Studies Exercise for Middle School Students." *Social Education*, 57(6), 1993, p. 337.

Hicks, Karen, & Jordan Austin. "Experiencing the Legal System: Fairy Tale Trials for Fifth Graders." *The Social Studies*, January–February 1994, pp. 39–43.

Holbrook, Hilary Taylor. "Writing to Learn in Social Studies." ERIC/RCS, 1988, pp. 217–218.

Kneeshaw, Stephen. "KISSing in the History Classroom: Simple Writing Activities That Work." *The Social Studies*, July–August 1992, pp. 176–179.

Lehning, James R. "Writing about History and Writing in History." *The History Teacher, 26*(3) May 1993, pp. 339–349.

McLeod, Jack R. "Creative Writing in the Social Studies." *Social Education*, November–December 1992, p. 398.

Miller, Etta, Luther B. Clegg, & Bill Vanderhoof. "Creating Postcards from the Famous for Social Studies Classes." *Journal of Reading, 36*(2), October 1992, pp. 134–135.

Myers, John W. *Writing to Learn across the Curriculum: Fastback 209.* Bloomington, IN: Phi Delta Kappa Educational Foundation, 1984.

O'Day, Kim. "Using Formal and Informal Writing in Middle School Social Studies." *Social Education, 58*(1), 1994, pp. 39–40.

Richburg, Robert W., Barbara J. Nelson, & Jennifer E. Reid. "Jump-Starting Thinking: Challenging Student Preconceptions." *The Social Studies*, March–April 1994, pp. 66–69.

Risinger, C. Frederick. *Current Directions in Social Studies.* ERIC Document Reproduction Service #ED 359130, 1992.

Rhoades, Lynn. "Quick Start Ideas for Teaching Current Events with Newspapers." *Social Education, 58*(3), 1994, p. 173.

Sturtevant, Elizabeth G. "Reading, Writing, and Experience in High School Social Studies and Science." *Contemporary Education, 65*(2) Winter 1994, pp. 95–98.

Sunal, Cynthia S., & Mary E. Haas. "Convincing American Women to Join in the Efforts to Win World War I: A Lesson Plan." *Social Education, 58*(2), 1994, pp. 89–91.

Winchell, Dick, & Dana Elder. "Writing in the Geography Curriculum." *Journal of Geography*, November–December 1994, pp. 273–276.

9

WRITING IN ART AND MUSIC

The two forms of expression, writing and visual imagery, do not depend on each other for a student to perform either. Nevertheless, I believe the two forms relate. Together they work to help the student analyze his or her role in the creative experience.
—*CONNIE HESS, 1992*

Prereading Questions

1. Art, music, and writing are all creative endeavors. What relationship do they have with the learning process?
2. What do you think a secondary student needs to learn in music and/or art classes?
3. What was your best and worst experience in art and music in middle and high school?
4. In what ways have you used writing in music and art?
5. How might music and art improve writing?

Introduction

In this chapter, we explore ways that writing is used to learn art and music. Writing plays an important role in helping students think about the fine arts, as well as helping them learn vocabulary and concepts. Karen Ernst, an art teacher, explains the close connection between art, writing, and learning:

> I believe in the value of focusing on the process; the idea that writing is a way of thinking and critical to any classroom or discipline; the idea that art is a way of knowing, of making meaning; and the idea that learning

from observing my students is a way to bring change to my classroom practice. (Ernst, 1994, p. 44)

The 1994 National Standards for Arts Education set guidelines for what students should know and be able to do by the time they graduate from high school.

- They should be able to communicate at a basic level in the four art disciplines—dance, music, theater, and the visual arts.
- They should be able to communicate proficiently in at least one art form.
- They should be able to develop and present basic analyses of works of art.
- They should have an informed acquaintance with exemplary works of art from a variety of cultures and historical periods.
- They should be able to relate various types of arts knowledge and skills within and across the arts.

Although there is a multitude of ways that these standards can be taught and learned, writing plays an important part in helping students and teachers achieve these five goals. Journal writing, comparison papers, vocabulary study, descriptions, explanations, how-to reports, and other writing activities are all important and appropriate components of the art and music curriculum. Several examples of writing to learn in art and music are illustrated in this chapter.

Writing in Art

Prior Experience Writing

A good place to introduce writing into the art classroom is with students writing their personal history of art experiences. A teacher may help the students think about their past experiences by asking questions. Do they enjoy art classes? What is their best experience related to art? Their worst? Has their interest grown or waned over the years? What do they most like to draw, paint, or sculpt? A class discussion should follow the writing activity so that students have an opportunity to share experiences. Because teachers are enthusiastic about their subject, it is difficult to remember that some of the students dislike or are actually fearful of art. By reading the personal histories, teachers discover how the students feel about art, and this helps teachers to structure activities that build confidence and, ultimately, enjoyment.

Writing as a Response to Art

Art institutes are a rich source of ideas for teaching art. Diane Levy of the Minneapolis Institute of Arts created a packet of ideas that incorporate writing into art activities. I have selected and adapted five of Levy's examples to illustrate a variety of possible choices.

1. Show the students *Olive Tree* by van Gogh and *Chestnut Trees at the Jas de Bouffan* by Cézanne. Students focus on details in a painting, by writing words that describe the trees in one of the paintings. Using these words, they then compose a sentence that describes the trees in the selected painting. Students read their sentence out loud and others guess which painting it refers to. The teacher leads a discussion helping students recognize additional details and how these, too, may be expressed in writing. Then students write a paragraph about the picture describing it in detail. This can also be done in groups rather than individually.

2. The following activity uses the same paintings, and the students make comparisons between the two. Each painting is examined for four elements: color, line, texture, and composition. Making a chart will facilitate their organization and writing.

	Van Gogh	*Cézanne*
Color		
Line		
Texture		
Composition		

Students draw conclusions about the total effect created by the combination of the four elements. The next writing activity is a comparison paper that should be at level 2 or 3. Students begin by comparing the effect of the paintings and then compare each of the elements to support their claim.

3. Another activity that encourages the skill of close observation is to use *Catskill Mountain House* by Cropsey. Because the painting depicts the landscape of the Catskill Mountains, students could think of the area as a vacation setting.

Their assignment is to write an advertisement for a travel magazine that would convince people to visit the area. To make the ad effective, details from the painting need to be included in the ad. To further the visual impact and the writing–art connection, the painting could be mounted on the wall with the ads clustered around it.

4. The painting *Still Life* by Claesz is an excellent starting place to encourage students to use figurative language. Using the five senses, one sense at a time, students write as many images as possible that describe items in the painting. For example, "Hear the steely knife scraping the crisp linen tablecloth" (Ernst, 1994, p. 13). Next, students create similes based on items in the painting and then write alliterations. Combining all the images they have composed, they write a poem of several stanzas.

5. Having students write a descriptive paragraph using *Death of Germanicus* by Poussin helps them to learn formal analysis of art. First, the students list the details in the painting; questions will help focus their attention:

- What colors has the artist used?
- What kinds of lines are present?
- What sense of texture is there?
- How are things distributed in space?

Using the notes they have compiled, students decide what idea they think the artist was trying to convey. This becomes the paragraph topic as they write a description of the scene. The activity helps to emphasize the importance of relevant examples.

Levy's examples could be used for many different paintings. The important point is that through writing in response to the visual aspect of art, the students learn more about art and how to express that knowledge through words. One could say the students are becoming artistically literate.

Writing and Art Activity

Esther E. Grisham of the Art Institute of Chicago also has several teaching suggestions that I have adapted. She selected four self-portraits by famous painters as a springboard for teaching ideas. The first portrait she suggests using is a self-portrait by Vincent van Gogh where his interest in the way colors reveal emotion and symbolic effects is strikingly evident (Grisham, 1993, p. 26). The classroom discussion focuses on how the colors used in the painting are related to the feelings evoked in the viewer. Grisham suggests having students write a letter to van Gogh each week describing in detail how they spend their time and what they are observing around them. Using mirrors, the students create a self-portrait each week to go along with their letter. They continue the letters and self-portraits over several weeks, experimenting with different media each time. The final activity is to have students make a self-portrait that expresses their personality through the combination of art, color, and writing.

The second portrait is by Ivan Albright and depicts the artist drinking wine at a table strewn with objects (p. 27). After a discussion of all the objects in the painting and what the objects tell the viewer about Albright, students make a list of their own favorite possessions and then choose the objects they think best describe their personalities. The students draw, paint, or create a collage of their favorite possessions, including their self-portrait.

The third painting, by Max Beckmann, "addresses the relationship of the artist to a world marked by the ideological turbulence that resulted in two world wars" (p. 38). Discussion of the self-portrait focuses on the background and his appearance, with special attention to his hands. Students are asked if his hands look real and what they think their significance is. Students think of a strong emotion that they would like to depict in a self-portrait. Then they sit across from each other and take turns making facial expressions that reflect the emotion they chose. They describe the changes in writing that occur in one's face as the emotions are displayed. Next they make self-portraits from a variety of angular shapes cut from construction paper. They finish the picture with markers, charcoal, and thick pencils. Students name the emotion shown in each other's work (p. 38).

The last self-portrait Grisham chose is by Beauford Delaney. The artist has "worked color, obvious brushwork, and texture onto the surface so that the artist's face looks almost like a craggy landscape, furrowed and rough" (p. 39). Following a discussion of the painting, students make a list of as many adjectives as they can that describe themselves, including physical characteristics and personality traits. With words from their lists, they make a self-portrait using the words themselves instead of lines. The words can be stretched or shortened, changed in any way to fit the needed lines and shapes. In these suggested activities, Grisham uses discussions, visualization, and writing to help students understand artists' work and to experiment themselves with a variety of styles and media.

A related activity designed by art teacher, Marla Shoemaker, helps students to recognize and understand realism in art. To begin, the students define what they think *realism* is. The teacher writes the definitions on a chalkboard or overhead while the students contribute as a group. She then shows the students *Prometheus Bound* by Rubens. First, the students rate how realistic the painting is, using 10 to mean totally realistic. She has the students describe what they see and asks them questions to make sure they notice all the important aspects. Shoemaker then tells them the myth of Prometheus. She divides the class in half with one group listing everything in the painting that is realistic and the other group listing the unrealistic. The students do not have to defend their selections; they are compiling data through their list making. The two groups then report to the whole class; discussion and argument follow as they debate which list a particular element belongs on. If necessary, the teacher helps the students see the exaggerated aspects such as the lighting. They discuss why Ruben painted this way. The students again rate the painting on how realistic it is. The activity helps students in art appreciation as well as encouraging them to use exaggeration and distortion in their own work.

Art History and Writing

Although art history is usually taught chronologically, it is often divorced from historical frames of reference. Students need to see works of art as part of a long tradition of art making (Stinespring & Steele, 1993, p. 7). Students could develop timelines connecting art with historical events (p. 8). Also, students can group works of art by visual characteristics and then "report on events within the world that may have influenced artists at the time" (p. 11). Learning about artwork within a historical context helps students understand, appreciate, and remember better.

Vocabulary for Art

Art critics and historians communicate ideas about art. They "discuss works of art in a certain way, using not only a familiar set of facts, but also a particular vocabulary and rhetoric that are both specialized and shared" (Murdick & Grinstead, 1992, p. 58). As teachers, we want our students to develop that ability, too. Depending on the particular art class and the level of students, the vocabulary would vary. However, a basic art vocabulary would include shape, form, line, color, texture, and perspective. Foremost, a teacher uses the vocabulary commonly in the context of discussing art with the students. Of course, a teacher can't assume all students are picking up on the meaning, but at least the words become familiar with the repetition. Giving an exam out of the context of works of art is a poor way to check on the students' knowledge of vocabulary. High school teacher Gary Bennett, as a way of checking his students' knowledge, has them describe pictures (1990, p. 151). One can easily see what words the students are comfortable using and then adjust teaching to emphasis the words not frequently used by students. Because the vocabulary is important for students to have the ability to articulate their knowledge and opinions, they need to use the language, not only hear the words.

In addition to learning vocabulary to discuss art in general, students use the specialized meanings to critique their own work. By knowing what to look for in other's work, they are able to examine their own work with more detail, rather than only with a comment on whether it's "good" or not. The written word helps them to improve their artistic skills through specificity. Students should always evaluate their own work as both process and product because this leads to new understanding. The writing helps them to reflect and can be used as part of their evaluation portfolio.

Art and Literature

Because of the expressive nature of art and literature, the two are natural companions; studying one enhances the study of the other. The units in an English class can form the basis for selecting works of art to study. A school district in California creates a mini-museum every year focusing on themes taught in literature classes. The project is intended for elementary levels and involves the visual arts coordinator, classroom teachers, and parents (Peshette, 1993, p. 28). An adaptation for secondary students is easily done by the art teacher alone but also could be taught cooperatively by the English and art teachers. In either case, the project begins with identifying literature themes. Examples might include family, searching for self, cultural norms, justice, and death and dying. Even if literature is not organized around themes, students can decide what themes are presented in the literature they have read. Themes from movies also work well. Students discuss the literature and begin selecting art prints they believe represent the same theme. They choose one print and create a presentation to share with the class. The presentation might include their own work using either the same theme or the same style of the famous artist. Also, information on the artist, his or her life and work, and an explanation of the style are included. The final projects are displayed on posters and placed in a prominent location, perhaps in a school hallway or a local art gallery. The combination of art, reading, and writing adds interest and depth for the students.

Emphasis and Allusion in Art

Pieter Brueghel's *Landscape with the Fall of Icarus* is an excellent painting for helping students recognize the use of background and foreground for emphasis; also, perspective is illustrated by the size and location of the figures. First they read or listen to the myth of Icarus and then discuss Brueghel's reading of the myth. They describe in detail each figure and how the figure contributes to what they think the painter is expressing.

Margaret Sims uses the same painting to help students understand allusion— that is, how incidental objects, colors, shadings, and so on add to the overall meaning that a viewer may acquire. Sims relates the painting to works in literature, and her students discuss the myth of Icarus as well as other selected works. Examples might include:

> W. H. Auden's "Musée des Beaux Arts"
> Edward Field's "Icarus"
> Anne Sexton's "To a Friend Whose Work Has Come to Triumph"
> William Carlos Williams's "Landscape with the Fall of Icarus"

As a concluding activity, students write a newspaper article which includes an allusion to the Icarus myth or write a poem using the myth or design a book jacket including a reference to the myth. Students learn how allusion adds depth to both paintings and literature (Sims, 1992, p. 87).

Types of Writing Appropriate in Art

As with other subjects, when writing in art classes, students need to use the three levels of writing and the three categories that James Britton and colleagues identified: expressive, transactional, and poetic. For example, if students are asked to write a critique of a painting, which is a transactional type of writing and probably a level 2, the first step would be a level 1 expressive assignment. For example, they write all the details they notice in the painting and also describe the effect the painting has for them. Doing so makes the critique more interesting and believable. "In the end, a scholarly analysis, if it is any good, reveals a personal vision" (Murdick & Grinstead, 1992, p. 60). We want students to go beyond their initial response, but if they don't begin with it, their writing lacks voice and becomes what they think the teacher wants. To become actively engaged in learning about art, they must include their personal responses.

A teacher, Rebecca Olien, compiled a list of activities for both expressive and expository (transactional) writing.

Expressive

1. Visit an art museum or show. Write about the piece(s) that most affected you, and explain in what way.
2. Write and illustrate a picture book for young children.
3. Illustrate a short story of your own creation, or exchange stories and illustrate your friend's.
4. Write evaluations of your own art project. Describe what you like about it and what leaves you dissatisfied.
5. Evaluate professional works of art and describe how a piece makes you feel.
6. Describe the type of art you most like and the art you dislike. Explain your reasons.

Expository

1. Write a report of a contemporary artist.
2. Report on a specific period of art history; include influences and development.
3. Compare and contrast techniques used and described for a particular mode of art as used by different artists.
4. Write a paper defining the difference between art and crafts; include examples of each.
5. Compare and contrast how artists express a similar theme.
6. Write a paper describing the major influences in art over the years.
7. Interview a professional artist and write up the interview.
8. Interview two artists and report on their similarities and differences.

Poetry and Art

Poetry and art seem a natural combination. Students can write a poem in the shape of an image, for instance, waves crashing on the shore or rain clouds darkening the sky. Also, students may use their artistic knowledge and sensory perception to write a poem about the shades and tone of a color. The poem could be either abstract or concrete. An example by eighth-grade student Jessica Olien is illustrated in Figure 9–1.

FIGURE 9-1

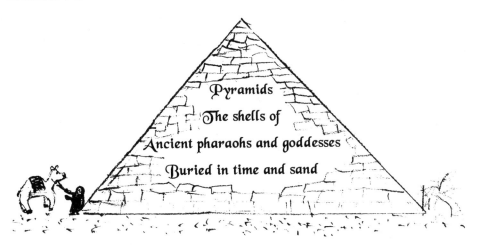

Pyramids
The shells of
Ancient pharaohs and goddesses
Buried in time and sand

Marilyn Bates, who teaches imaginative writing, developed an activity that uses art as a catalyst to poetry. The first step is to have the whole class view a slide that can evoke speculation; *The Scream* by Edvard Munch is a good example. The class as a whole offers comments and observations. The teacher can encourage the students to respond more fully by asking probing questions (Bates, 1993, p. 42).

Is there a central focus to the painting?
How does the use of colors direct your attention?
What mood does the painting project?
If you were going to retitle this work, what might you call it?

The teacher's goal is to keep the discussion going and to encourage the students to notice details. It is important to reassure the students that there is no one right way to interpret the painting, nor is there a right meaning. Following the class activity, students write their own journal entry about their reaction to the painting. "They may write anything they want, responding to the emotional message or merely describing the various images in the work of art" (Bates, 1993, p. 42). The next step is for students to write a poetic response based on their journal writing, including as many concrete details as possible. "This attention to detail increases their awareness of the various elements of the work, such as line, color, texture and shape . . ." (p. 42). After students write their poems and share them, a teacher might introduce some poets' work written in response to an artwork— for example, Williams Carlos Williams's "The Dance," written in response to Brueghel's *The Kermess*. The next step is for students to make their own selection of a work of art and follow the same procedure as they did in the class activity. The students' poems will reflect their understanding of the art and how it relates to personal experiences.

Journal Articles and Writing Activities

Articles published in art journals suggest topics for reports appropriate for older students' writing. As an example, an article appearing in *ArtNews,* "Who Are the Most Underrated and Overrated Artists?," contained the responses to that question from several art directors and curators. Using the article as a starting point, students could write their own response to the question in the same fashion by explaining their choice. They could select from contemporary or classical pieces. Such an activity would help them to think about their artistic tastes and learn how to defend their choices (Gardner, 1994).

Nancy Stapen's article "Who Are the Women Old Masters?" also is an appropriate basis for students exploring a topic and writing an informed report. Stapen describes the lives and work of several women artists from the sixteenth century to more modern times. She provides the background necessary for students to write an in-depth article on a subject they probably know little about.

A third article that provides the basis for a research report is "Images of Women in the Visual Media" by Sheri Klein. She examines the images of women depicted in cartoons and comics because, as she explains, both "have multicultural and socially relevant content" (Klein, 1993, p. 60). Students could compare how the images of women have changed over time or compare them with present-day male images found in cartoons and comics.

Writing and Artistic Activities

Because writing enhances thinking, we want students to write about their own artistic projects as well. By writing about their own work, they are able to achieve a more objective view and, consequently, understand how to improve their work.

- To begin, they can write an explanation of their own work of art: how they did it, what it represents, what mood they hope to project.
- They might write a how-to paper on firing a pot, or mixing colors, drawing perspective, or any one of the techniques they learn. An oral presentation based on the paper is a good follow-up.
- Writing about problems students encounter in their work helps them and their teacher know best how to overcome obstacles.
- A written description of a scene may later be the impetus for a picture. The notes can be quite detailed descriptions or just a few lines about a color, shadow, or movement. An artist notebook can be the source of many ideas for art work.

In summary, writing in art includes expressive, transactional, and poetic forms. Writing aids in students' understandings of artwork, helps tap their own creativity, and creates connections between the art and their own experiences.

Writing in Music

The National Standards for Arts Education lists nine content standards for music in grades 9–12. The first five cover performance, creating, and other elements of musical proficiencies; the last four focus on evaluation and analysis. The standards emphasize that every music course, including performance courses, should provide instruction in listening to and analyzing music in addition to teaching the subject matter. The music activities in this section are intended to help with the teaching and learning of the following content standards:

- Listening to, analyzing, and describing music
- Evaluating music and music performances
- Understanding relationships between music, the other arts, and disciplines outside the arts
- Understanding music in relation to history and culture

Standards in Music Classes

By the use of metaphors, Michael Masterson, a music professor, has designed activities that touch on all of the standards listed above. Because "insightful student responses to both familiar and unfamiliar music are what music teachers, particularly music appreciation teachers, desire from their students," he suggests having students listen carefully to a variety of compositions (Masterson, 1994, p. 24). Students need to have opportunities to discuss the feelings that the music provokes for them and then write how aspects of music connect with their responses. Although music is an important part of most young people's lives, they lack the language to express their thoughts about music. By using metaphors, they learn "how sounds, culture, and feelings connect in a musical performance" (p. 25). Connecting responses with metaphors gives them concrete and familiar images to explain their personal responses. Masterson, as an example, has students listen to Aaron Copland's "Fanfare for the Common Man" but does not tell them the title. He lists the musical elements on the board: melody, rhythm, harmony, timbre, texture, and form. As the students listen, they write down what instruments are playing, draw melodic shapes, and jot down feelings and associations that come to mind. As students share their responses, he writes them on the board alongside the elements. By asking questions, he helps his students begin to see the connections between feelings and musical sounds. He may start with the element of timbre by asking "What is a trumpet's color?" "What does a trumpet symbolize?" For texture he may ask what the foreground, middle ground, and background sounds are, or "What shape does the melody have?" (p. 26). The discussions continue, connecting all of the elements to the students' responses. The questions broaden so that students consider the implication of the social world and what story is being told. This method works for all types of music and provides vocabulary and understandings for students to talk about music.

Other teachers, too, use questions to help students think about the connections between their responses and the structural forms of music. Jeffrey Aaron provides an example using Act III of Wagner's *Lohengrin.* After listening closely to the selection, students write in their journals what they felt and thought. Then Aaron asks specific questions, for example, "How many times do we hear the powerful low-pitch theme in the first large section?" He leads the students into a discussion linking their answers to their responses so that they understand how the music achieves a particular effect (p. 35).

Other suggestions for journal writing include:

1. What role does music play in my life?
2. My least favorite piece of music is _____ , and explain why in specific terms.
3. My favorite composer is _____ because . . .
4. When I'm sad (or happy, or angry, or any other emotion), I like to listen to or play (list names of compositions).
5. Keep a list for one week of all the places you hear music. Write about your reaction to what you heard.

The journal writing described above is expressive in nature. As stated in the section on writing in art, James Britton's categories—expressive, transactional, and poetic—are all appropriate for music classes; in fact, it is essential that teachers use all three modes. Rebecca Olien, a teacher, has compiled a list of activities for music that includes expressive and expository (transactional).

Expressive
1. Keep a record of how often you hear music and how it affects you throughout the day (in grocery stores, elevators, stores, etc.).
2. Write descriptions of moods that different pieces of music create in you.
3. Picture yourself in a place as you listen to music. Write a description of that place.
4. Compose lyrics to a musical score.
5. Write a story to be recorded in which music is intertwined throughout the reading.

Expository
1. Describe the process of making a particular instrument.
2. Trace types of music (rock, blues, jazz, etc.) from its origins. Find samples that correspond to the periods of development.
3. Write a biography of a musician, composer, or conductor.
4. Sit in on a practice and performance of a band, choir, or orchestra. If possible, interview a member. Write a paper describing what it would be like to be a member.
5. Write a report on the music of other cultures.
6. Describe the influences of present day music.

Music and Social Change

A middle school teacher, Judy Foust (1990), uses her students' strong feelings about fairness to help them discover the power of words and music that can activate social change. She introduces a wide range of protest songs: "After the Buffalo's Gone," "Blowin' in the Wind," "Sounds of Silence," and "Brick in the Wall." First, the students read the lyrics as poetry; then she plays the recordings. The students bring in additional protest songs and discuss how the tone of the music relates to the issue being protested. They listen for volume, speed, major and minor notes, and other aspects of the composition. The class then brainstorms any present-day issues involving unfairness. Following the class discussion, students think of one or two issues they would like to write about.

Working in small groups, the students use the following format to decide on one protest idea:

The problem:
Why is it unfair?
Examples?
How can it be changed or improved?

The students discuss melodies and the impact of the combination of words and music. Each group writes lyrics for the protest issue the members decided on. They sing the songs aloud and change the words as they work on rhythm patterns. When ready, each group sings its song for the rest of the class, and each song is recorded. The printed versions of the songs are collected in a class book.

To help students better understand and analyze the impact of a song, teachers have students listen carefully to a small selection of songs and decide on the theme of each one. Students also have the printed lyrics. Then they analyze why they came to the conclusion they did by considering the words and melody. What would change the theme? Students read a variety of poems looking for examples of the same themes as the songs. What type of music would enhance the theme of the poetry? This same activity can focus on the mood of a song rather than the theme.

Another suggestion for combining music and poetry is for students to add music to their own original poems. After they write and revise the poem, they decide on the music and movement to use. They may use instruments, pantomime, rhythmic movement, introductions, codas, ostinati, melody, and vocal expression. Each poem is performed for the rest of the class (Basile, 1994, p. 58).

As a rule teenagers have strong opinions about the type of music and the particular songs they like. We can sharpen their analytical skills by asking them to compare a song they like very much with one they do not care for. The two should be in the same general classification: classical, country, rock, heavy metal, rap, or any other general description. After a group discussion, the students write a paper defending their choice and explaining why they like one and not the other.

Music and Writing Children's Books

Students can write a children's book based on a story they derive from listening to program music (Kite, Smucker, Steiner, & Bayne, 1994). First, students listen several times to a selection of program music, for instance Aaron Copland's *Appalachian Spring Concert Suite,* Paul Dukas's *The Sorcerer's Apprentice,* George Gershwin's *An American in Paris,* or another selection (p. 34). As they listen, the students visualize images and record them in their journal. After repeating this several times, they develop a story line that the music suggests to them. They use the musical comparatives to guide the story; when the music is slow, so is the action. Using beat, meter, rhythm, and melody, they interact the story with the musical elements and create an interwoven piece. If possible, the students can play the music and read the book to children of the age the book is intended for.

Summary

The activities described above are only a small sampling of the many possibilities for combining writing and music. Writing helps students learn that music and art are basic forms of communication and that we can learn about ourselves and other people of the world by exploring our thoughts and feelings through the process of writing.

Discussion Questions

1. What are the connections between studying about art and creating art? Where does writing tie the two together?
2. In what ways could writing help personalize art critiquing?
3. How could writing help a student improve artistically? How could art help improve writing?
4. In what ways do music and writing enhance the study of each?
5. In what ways will you include writing in your music or art classes?

Suggested Activities

1. Select one or two additional paintings that a teacher could use for the activities Levy (1985) suggests, or select music for the activities Masterson (1994) describes.
2. Devise writing activities that would help students learn an element of art or of music.
3. Working in small groups, create a unit that combines art and music. Include writing activities that help students succeed in reaching the goals of the unit.
4. Choose a musical selection and write discussion questions for students that would help them understand the connections between their personal feelings and associations and the musical elements.

5. Keep a music or art journal for a week. Write down every place you encounter music or art, and write your reactions to what you see or hear. What impact do they have on your life?

References

Aaron, Jeffrey. "Integrating Music with Core Subjects." *Music Educators Journal, 80*(6), May 1994, pp. 33–36.

Basile, Donna. "Music and Poetry." *Music Educators Journal, 80*(4), January, 1994, p. 58.

Bates, Marilyn. "Imitating the Greats: Art as the Catalyst in Student Poetry." *Art Education, 46*(4), July 1993, pp. 41–45.

Bennett, Gary. "Language and the Teaching of Art." *Educational Research, 32,*(2) Summer 1990, pp. 150–154.

Caldwell, Helen, & Blaine H. Moore. "The Art of Writing: Drawing as Preparation for Narrative Writing in the Primary Grades." *Studies in Art Education, 32,*(4), 1991, pp. 207–219.

Ernst, Karen. "Writing Pictures, Painting Words: Writing in an Artists' Workshop." *Language Arts, 71,* January 1994, pp. 44–52.

Foust, Judy. "Writing under Protest." Unpublished paper, 1990.

Gardner, Paul. "Who Are the Most Underrated and Overrated Artists?" *Art News, 93*(2), February 1994, pp. 110–113.

Grisham, Esther E. "Four Self-Portraits." *Art Education, 46*(4) July 1993, pp. 26–28+.

Hess, Connie. "Visual Expression and Writing." *Arts & Activities,* January 1992, p. 42.

Kite, Thomas S., Thomas Smucker, Stan Steiner, & Mina Bayne. "Using Program Music for Interdisciplinary Study." *Music Educators Journal, 80*(5), March 1994, pp. 33–36+.

Klein, Sheri. "Images of Women in the Visual Media." *Art Education, 46*(5), September 1993, pp. 60–65.

Levy, Diane. "Reading, Writing, and Art for Secondary Students." Minneapolis Institute of Arts, 1985.

Masterson, Michael L. "Moving Beyond It's Got a Good Beat." *Music Educators Journal, 80*(6), May 1994, pp. 24–28.

Murdick, William, & Richard Grinstead. "Art, Writing, and Politics." *Art Education,* September 1992, pp. 58–65.

National Standards for Arts Education. Consortium of National Arts Education Associations, 1994.

Peshette, Alix. "A Thousand Words Are Worth a Picture." *Arts & Activities,* January 1993, pp. 28–29.

Shoemaker, Marla K. "Helping Adolescents Look at Art." *School Arts, 83*(7), 1984, pp. 25–27.

Sims, Margaret C. "Brueghel Teaches Allusion." *English Journal,* November 1992, p. 87.

Stapen, Nancy. "Who Are the Women Old Masters?" *Art News, 93*(4), March 1994, pp. 87–94.

Stinespring, John A., & Brian D. Steele. "Teaching Art History: Getting Started." *Art Education, 46*(2), March 1993, pp. 7–13.

10

EVALUATION OF WRITING

No matter how trustworthily we may evaluate any sample of a student's writing, we lose all the trustworthiness if we go on to infer from just that one sample the student's actual skill in writing.—PETER ELBOW, 1987, P. 221

Prereading Questions

1. In what ways may your own writing assignments have been evaluated unfairly?
2. What kind of evaluation is the most help in improving your writing?
3. Has your perception of the quality of your work ever differed greatly from that of a teacher?
4. What do you see as the greatest difficulty in evaluating the writing of your future students?
5. What is the relationship between evaluation and teaching?

Introduction

We evaluate to discover what our students are learning and also how effective our teaching is. How we evaluate is at the crux of our teaching and cannot be added on as an afterthought. Evaluation of student work has always been a major concern for teachers, students, and parents. Concern about fairly representing students' effort and growth, as well as their final outcome, makes evaluation a difficult part of our teaching. And we worry about evaluation actually helping students improve. For students, uncertainty about what grade they will receive gives them a sense of powerlessness and frustration. Too often, grades are in conflict with both teachers' and students' expectations. Additionally, when writing is a major part of the teaching and learning in a classroom, the workload of keeping up with student papers can become overwhelming for teachers. Evaluation cannot be left to chance. To develop fair and consistent policies, teachers need to follow guidelines like these:

1. Evaluation must fit the purpose of each assignment.
2. Many types of evaluation are appropriate.
3. Students must be involved in the evaluation.

Evaluation and Purpose

Purpose and evaluation of a writing assignment go hand in hand through implementation of levels of writing. The chapter on levels discussed the variety of assignments we use throughout the writing process. As a review, brief summaries of the levels follow: Level 1 is used for informal writing such as discovery activities and journal writing, writing designed for practice and getting thoughts on paper. Level 2 is appropriate for homework, exams, and the majority of classroom writing. Level 3 is for students' "best writing" and is often intended for a wider audience.

Level 1 writing is not evaluated except occasionally, in an informal way, and only content is considered. Level 2 writing is usually evaluated. The emphasis is mainly on content, with some attention to writing conventions. Level 3 writing is evaluated more stringently, with a focus on both content and writing skills

The appropriate level for each activity is determined by the purpose of the assignment. If the writing is for practice, it is a level 1 and, therefore, either is not evaluated at all or is read quickly to see if a student is developing the particular skill. The teacher can then add a comment to let students know if they are doing all right. Other purposes for level 1 assignments are developing fluency, trying out ideas, organizing thoughts, and experimenting with a variety of forms and styles. Formal evaluation of writing activities that reflect these purposes is not appropriate, although teachers will want to know how students are doing.

If the purpose of an assignment is to help students develop their own voice and style in writing, then the evaluation is concerned only with a student experimenting with voice and style, and actually requires no formal evaluation. If the purpose is to learn how to take notes, then, again, no teacher evaluation is appropriate. Students will know through peer interaction during group work if they are learning the skill of note-taking and how to improve. The same is true when students are gathering their thoughts about prior knowledge or reviewing information before taking a test. In other words, when the purpose of the activity is to provide guided opportunities for practice, formal evaluation interferes with the purpose.

The purpose for a writing activity can be quite specific. A teacher may want students to learn how to use a variety of sentence patterns in order to make their writing more interesting and to connect thoughts in ways that provide meaning for the reader. After a few short lessons on semicolons, subordination, coordination, and wordiness, the teacher designs an activity with the purpose of using a variety of sentences. Students write a short paper on an appropriate topic, depending on the class, and include a variety of sentences to connect ideas. The teacher evaluates the papers on how well the sentence variety adds interest and meaning. This type of activity is at level 2.

Similar activities focus on summarizing material from the student text, writing an annotated bibliography, using reference material to back up major points, and organizing material from more than one source. All these activities help prepare students for more formal report writing. Students need an opportunity to practice, and this type of assignment provides that. The practice, however, is specific, follows informational lessons, and, therefore, calls for evaluation.

The more formal style of level 3 requires a more formal evaluation. One purpose of a level 3 assignment is to pull together a documented report or research paper; or students might write a piece for publication, such as a poem, letter, or report. The audience for published work is not only wider but might be largely unknown, as is the case with writing for scholarships, job applications, or contest submissions. Only one's best writing is suitable for publication beyond the classroom; therefore, multiple drafting, revising, editing, and proofreading are all required.

To sum up, evaluation varies with the purpose of the assignment. Once a teacher determines the "why" of an assignment, the level of writing is apparent, and the type of appropriate evaluation is clear.

Types of Evaluation

Informal

Teachers can keep in touch with students' work using informal methods. For instance, when students are sharing level 1 writing in a group, the teacher needs to circulate around the room stopping by one group and moving on to another. When students are involved in group work, the teacher is not the focal point of the activity; however, he or she is still involved and interested in what is going on. Some teachers use group time to take care of other tasks, but this can be interpreted by the students as a lack of interest on the part of the teacher. On the other hand, a teacher does not want to direct group interaction by taking over discussion. With practice and awareness teachers can achieve a balance between too much and too little involvement.

When teachers are circulating among groups, stopping to listen to a discussion or to a student reading from a journal or notes, their awareness of how the students are progressing is heightened. A few notes jotted down help teachers to check later with individual students who are not doing as well as they could. It is a mistake for teachers to collect these papers "just to read over quickly" because, once they are handed in, students will expect some written comment, if not a grade, to show what the teacher thought of their work. Not only are teachers taking on unnecessary work, but they are defeating the purpose of level 1 assignments. Student writers will not experiment with voice and style if their papers are to be evaluated. Throughout their years in school, they have become too grade-conscious to take chances.

Self-Evaluation

Self-evaluation is of primary importance, for two reasons. First, we want students to acknowledge responsibility for their writing. If they have problems with an assignment or do not understand the directions, the students themselves need to seek help. Also, they are responsible for making sure they receive the needed assistance with revision. This is assuming that the teacher creates a classroom atmosphere that provides opportunities for students to interact with other students and conference with other students and the teacher.

The second reason is that if the writing does not please the writer, it most likely will not please anyone else. Too often, students react to evaluation as if they have no say in the matter—almost as if they did not write the piece and have no concept of how evaluation is related to what they wrote. Students need to be involved in the whole writing process, including evaluation.

Evaluating one's own writing is not an easy task. Some techniques can help, but one that is *not* helpful is a checklist. Checklists are designed to help students think about particular areas, but they are too general to help much and do not require a thoughtful response. When we look at a list of yes/no questions about our writing, it is too easy to simply answer "yes." For example, a list commonly includes questions like this: Is every word spelled correctly? Are main ideas supported? Is the paper well organized? Is your word choice correct and appropriate? Most, if not all, students would answer "yes" to all of these. None of these questions calls for a thoughtful response. Throughout this book, the role of students as active learners is stressed. Evaluation is no exception.

How, then, do we get students to view their own writing objectively? Some strategies can help students focus on their own writing.

• Before bringing their draft to the response group for the first time, students read their paper aloud to themselves. Hearing the words rather than only seeing them, helps highlight awkward phrasing. Perhaps words are repeated too often, or words are left out, or the rhythm of the spoken sentences illustrates a tendency to overuse the same sentence pattern.

• After reading their papers aloud, students revise their work. Revisions may look informal because at this stage in the writing process no one but the writer sees the paper. The important part is that the revisions are made and writers do not explain away problem areas while reading the paper to the group members.

FIGURE 10-1   Self-Evaluation Form

Name of paper _____

Date I read it aloud and made revisions

Signed _____

- Students fill in a form, noting the date they revised their own paper, and sign their name (Figure 10–1).

The completed form becomes part of the packet for the writing assignment. Students are reminded of this step and tend to take it more seriously when they are required to formalize their self-assessment.

Questions can focus students on particular areas of their writing and help with the self-evaluation process. Because the questions depend on the assignments and the students' ages, the following questions serve only as guidelines:

Where do I need to add support for main points?
Where would details make the meaning more clear to a reader?
What information would strengthen my paper?
How can I make the paper more interesting?

Impression Grading

When teachers evaluate students' work to get a quick sense of how the students are doing, they use impression grading. A quick read-through tells them if students are catching on to the concepts, understanding the assignment, putting forth effort, and actively involved in the activity. Letter grades are not appropriate for this type of evaluation; teachers write comments and/or use a check mark system. "Good work. Keep going" encourages students and reassures them they are doing okay. Other comments relate to areas that are especially weak or strong. The comments are meant to guide students' work and, therefore, need to be specific. The following statements are examples of what kind of comments help students.

"Your statements are too general."
"Explain why this is true."
"Check the textbook on this. You have misconceptions here."
"You need to include more detail. Your meaning is not clear."
"A good start, but the rest seems hurried and not thought out."

The more specific teachers are, the more guidance the students have. That's true for positive statements, too.

"Good use of detail here."
"Sequence is very clear."
"You selected the important points."

Most students have a combination of areas that need more work or that are fine, and that is why specific remarks help the most.

Impression grading works best for assignments that call on students to summarize what they read or what they heard in a lecture. A teacher might ask students to write a paragraph on what they learned after studying a particular topic. The purpose of such assignments is to do a quick check of students' understanding. Although a test at the end of a unit might tell a teacher the same thing, the information comes after the fact and is of little help in furthering students' learning.

Impression grading takes little of the teacher's time. Because the evaluation is focused on general understanding, the teacher needs only to skim the writing, reading as quickly as possible. Also, the impression grade is rarely recorded, although occasionally a teacher may want to record it to document growth and change in a student's work. When they are recorded, the check marks serve as a general impression of the student's work.

√+   good understanding, progressing well
√   doing O.K., no serious problems
√–   does not show understanding, needs help
0   did not do the work

Teachers need to remember, though, that few of the assignments that call for impression grading require keeping a record of the grade. Recording takes time and should not occur without a specific purpose. Evaluation is to help students know how they are doing while in the process of learning. Teachers record grades in order to report on a student's progress over a period of time, usually nine to eighteen weeks. In that length of time, most teachers accumulate an abundance of grades that represent progress. In other words, teachers do not record every grade.

Analytical Grading Scales

Analytical grading scales, usually referred to just as grading scales, break down the total number of points possible for a writing assignment into divisions according to the areas of writing competencies. The parts of a written piece are evaluated, and the grades for each part are added up for a total grade. They are analytical in the sense that a teacher analyzes the paper according to the areas in the scale. Students know how their grade reflects what they did, and teachers know they are balancing the elements of writing in a fair and unbiased way.

The scales were developed by Paul Diederich and his associates at the Educational Testing Service for the purpose of scoring SAT essays. Although the scale is no longer used for the SAT readings, the format is useful to classroom teachers for grading papers that have gone through the writing process, usually level 3 papers. Diederich's scale is in Figure 10–2.

Two general principles are apparent in the Diederich scale. One is that the criteria for evaluation need to be clearly defined, and the other is that each criterion has a point value assigned according to its importance. Although the criteria and point value may differ widely from one assignment to another, these two principles guide the construction of all grading scales.

The criteria represent the basis of the evaluation and differ depending on the purpose of the activity. For example, if the assignment is to write a lab report in science, the scale might include a record of observed information, a list of material used, procedures followed, and interpretation of results, as well as use of details, clear explanations, and organization. Next, teachers assign point values to the list of criteria according to the value of each in the total evaluation.

An example of a writing activity in history or social studies illustrates what a scale may look like in Figure 10–3. Figure 10–4 is an example of an analytical scale used for a report that required references.

The analytical scale can reflect recent areas of study or review. For example, if the students are working on using a greater variety of sentences, then that appears on the grading scale. The same is true for paragraph cohesion, details to support claims, or introductions and conclusions. Point value can adapt to class-work, also. At one time spelling may carry a point value of 2, at another time a 5, depending on the importance of spelling in a particular activity. Or the point

---

FIGURE 10-2   Diederich Scale

Quality and development of ideas	1	2	3	4	5	
Organization, relevance, movement	1	2	3	4	5	
						_____ × 5 =
Style, flavor, individuality	1	2	3	4	5	
Wording and phrasing	1	2	3	4	5	
						_____ × 3 =
Grammar, sentence structure	1	2	3	4	5	
Punctuation	1	2	3	4	5	
Spelling	1	2	3	4	5	
Manuscript form, legibility	1	2	3	4	5	
						_____ × 1 =

FIGURE 10-3   A Comparison Paper (30 points)

	Possible Points	Your Points
Thesis and introduction:	2	_____
Takes a stand		
Clear what paper is about		
Major points:	8	_____
Consistent		
Easy to follow		
Supporting details:	12	_____
For every major point		
Examples		
Quotes or paraphrases		
Organization:	5	_____
For whole essay		
Paragraph-level		
Conclusion		
Punctuation, spelling, word usage	3	_____
Comments:		

Your total points _____

---

value may go up because students are careless. An increased point value helps to direct their attention to a problem area, although a balance among the writing elements needs to be maintained. Too high a percentage of points for any one element turns the writing activity into a skill exercise and does not give credit to the student's effort and ability.

The major advantage of analytical scales for students is that they know why they receive the grade they do. Students have difficulty comparing circled errors, positive comments like "good point," and negative comments like "not clear," which all add up in the end to a "B." If we want evaluation to help students improve their writing, they have to know exactly why and how a teacher arrived at the grade.

Scoring guides help teachers grade quickly, precisely, and honestly. As teachers read a student's paper, they write evaluative comments on the guide, not on the paper itself. For writing conventions, it is simply a matter of keeping track of misspellings, comma errors, run-on sentences, and so on. For content-related areas, a teacher writes comments on the guide in the appropriate place. The comments reflect both areas for improvement and praise for doing well. The scoring guide is gradually filled in as the teacher reads the paper. Teachers do not have to keep considering the grade as they read, but they come to a realization of the overall effect of the paper. In general, does the writing accomplish what it should? Are the style and voice appropriate for the assignment? When

FIGURE 10-4   Research Paper: "Careers"
(Grading Sheet)

	Possible Points	Your Points
1. Introduction Connections between self and career; enough detail and explanation	5	
2. Subquestions Adequate covering of topic	4	
3. Support of questions Enough detail, explanation	5	
4. References Introduced, clear where they came from, who they are	5	
5. Interviews Responses clear, incorporated	5	
6. Conclusion Pulls paper together, strong, thoughtful	3	
7. Spelling	5	
8. Punctuation MLA style throughout, including references	10	
9. Word usage Redundancies, grammar, connotation, specific	5	
10. Transitions Between paragraphs	3	

TOTAL POINTS

Comments:

teachers finish reading the student paper, they first figure the points for each category based on the notes they jotted down, and then add up the total number the student earned. General comments at the bottom of the sheet help direct students to areas they should work on, or praise for an area that is especially well written.

Analytical scales work well with papers that go through the entire writing process; however, a modified form of the scale is often used for papers that fall into the level 2 category. For these papers, fewer points are given to writing conventions such as punctuation, spelling, and format. A scale for a level 2 assignment might look like the one in Figure 10–5.

Figure 10–5 is a grading scale for an assignment appropriate for any subject: art, music, physical education, health, industrial arts, or any other. Students read three or more articles about an issue or a topic. They first locate appropriate articles following the guidelines the teacher provides. Next they read and paraphrase each article. This assignment follows classwork on note-taking and paraphrasing. Students then compare the information among the articles and write a conclusion based on their findings. The drafts are shared in response groups and students have the opportunity to revise. The purpose of the assignment is to put into practice the skills they worked on previously, as well as to understand the importance of comparing different viewpoints on an issue. The paper is worth 30 points, and the point distribution represents the purposes of the assignment.

Because purposes vary from one assignment to another, teachers must design analytical scales to fit each one. Of course, similarities exist from one to another, but generic scales do not represent the expected outcome nor the teacher's purpose. Also, generic scales do not allow for student input.

Student Involvement in Evaluation

How their work is evaluated should never come as a surprise to students. They need to know the level of the writing activity before they begin. Knowing the level

---

FIGURE 10-5   Level 2 Scale

Paraphrasing for the summaries	6	_____
Summaries capture pertinent points	5	_____
Articles appropriate for topic	3	_____
Comparisons among summaries consistent and clear	8	_____
Conclusion reflects the findings	5	_____
Mechanics and spelling	3	_____

also tells them what they need to pay attention to as they work on the writing. When analytic scales are used, they are available to students when the revising work begins. By having the grading scale well in advance of writing the final draft, students know what the teacher's expectations are, taking away the mystery of what is evaluated, and how.

In addition to knowing teacher expectations, students can also become involved in decisions regarding writing levels and development of grading scales. First, however, students need to become accustomed to the idea of establishing levels and scales. The best way to involve students in evaluations is for the teacher always to explain why an assignment is at a particular level and why the distribution of points fits the activity. Students have a right to know how their work will be evaluated. Also, by explaining the process to students, teachers help them to understand that grading is not arbitrary. Teachers often clarify their own thinking when they explain to students why a piece is graded in a particular way.

Once students are familiar with levels and grading scales, they can play an active part in establishing evaluation guidelines. First, the teacher explains the purpose of the assignment. Students interpret the purpose as "Why do we have to do this?" They should know why, even though they may not always agree that it is a worthwhile reason. Such explanations help bridge the gap between teacher and students because classrooms are often perceived as places where the teacher knows all the answers and the students do what they are told without knowing why.

When the teacher lays out the purpose for an assignment, there is not much disagreement about levels, although sometimes students argue for a level 2 to become a level 1. Students' reasons must make sense, and the teacher must consider them seriously. Not uncommonly, students will put more effort into an assignment when they succeed in convincing the teacher to change the level because of the sense of empowerment they have gained.

To get student input for analytic scales, the teacher goes over the purposes of the assignment and the recent classroom work that prepared students for the assignment. Using an overhead or the chalkboard, the teacher writes down what the students think should be included in the evaluation. No point values are assigned at this stage, just what should be considered as a reflection of the writing activity. The suggestions are grouped into a manageable number, and then point values are designated. The teacher usually decides on the total number of points, but that, too, can be changed. Students are not shy about expressing their ideas and opinions and usually get into lively discussions. The teacher has input, also, and the final criteria are negotiated among students and between students and teacher.

Soliciting student input and paying attention to it greatly reduces the feeling that grading is impersonal and unfair. Different classes will have slightly different scales, but the total point value should stay the same from one class to another. Scales with different total points would add to a teacher's burden, which is not the desired outcome for using analytical scales.

Portfolios, in particular, include student involvement. By design, they are collaborative in nature. Portfolios have three essential characteristics: longitudinal, diverse, and collaborative (Yancey, 1992, p. 102). Writers see their own development and can select assignments that best reflect what they have learned. Also, in writing their goals for the coming weeks, they are involved in what they want to learn, not always what a teacher says they should learn.

Portfolios

Although the idea of portfolios is not new, only recently have they caught on for classroom use. Although there may be a use for portfolios in large-scale testing, I am concerned here only with portfolios as part of the ongoing process of students and teachers involved in evaluation. Too often, we are judged on a one-time performance: a major test, a formal essay, one writing sample. The effort that went into the final product goes unnoticed, or the possibility that one had a bad day is ignored. Portfolios allow us to look at improvement over time and at the process of learning that led up to the final product.

Peter Elbow supports the idea of portfolios because they reinforce a continuing effort and improvement. Students are encouraged to revise and improve poor work rather than give up trying. They are more apt to "try for what is exciting, not just what's acceptable" (Elbow, 1991, p. 167). Students who feel free to take chances work harder to do their best.

Elbow explains that portfolios could be called "collaborative grading" (Belanoff & Dickson, 1991, p. xi). They give students the chance to show their "best" work, but also to say, "Look how hard I worked" or "See how much I accomplished." Consequently, they provide a better picture of student abilities than a test or one piece of writing.

A portfolio represents a student's work and is suitable for any course. We tend to think of portfolios as a collection of best work, much like what an artist carries to an interview for a job or a showing. But portfolios include much more than samples of one's best work; they also document students' growth and risk-taking. They represent what teachers want to measure—growth and development.

Portfolios can vary depending on the teacher and the class. Some are neatly created notebooks; others have many entries that are bulky and are stuffed in an expandable file; some are austere-looking; still others are covered with student artwork. Whatever their appearance inside and out, they all share a common philosophy: We value what students are achieving, their efforts and results, products and process, diversity and standards (Tierney, Carter, & Desal, 1991, p. 49).

Margie Krest, a high school teacher, has her students keep all of the writing in their portfolio, "including drafts, revisions, prewriting material, and final papers" (Krest, 1990, p. 29). Krest devised a method for evaluating that rewards the discovery activities, multiple drafts, revising, and all the practice vital to a well-written final paper. Students' work is ungraded until the whole portfolio is evaluated. Then she gives two grades for the portfolio, one for all of the writing and another for one of the final papers. She weighs the two grades depending on what she wants to emphasize. If fluency is of primary importance, the first grade might count for 75 percent and the final paper grade for 25 percent. On the other hand, she might reverse those percentages for a senior class (Krest, 1990, p. 31).

A teacher may use portfolios for different purposes throughout a semester or year, or teachers may use them in different ways. High school teacher Roberta J. Herter uses portfolio evaluation for a "fuller picture of a writer's growth over time" (Herter, 1991, p. 90). Also, students take a more active part in accepting responsibility for their writing.

> Portfolios involve students in assessing the development of their writing skills by inviting self-reflection and encouraging students to assume control over their writing. Accumulating a body of work to return to, to reject, revise, or simply revisit calls on students to become responsible for the content and quality of their portfolio, and ultimately to confront their personal writing inventories and investments in activities of the class. (Herter, 1991, p. 90)

When students have the choice to decide what goes into the portfolio, they are assuming some control over their evaluation, something that does not happen in many classrooms. The more we allow students a say in their evaluation, the more responsible they become. Feelings of powerlessness can cause problems of discipline and apathy.

In *Portfolio News*, Martha Johnson, director of a cooperative writing program, names several attitudes and behaviors that portfolios encourage in students (Johnson, 1991, p. 2).

- To take more responsibility for their work
- To see themselves as apprentices
- To value daily work as a meaningful part of learning
- To see mistakes as opportunities for learning
- To see revision as an opportunity to succeed
- To spend more time thinking about their teacher's response
- To spend more time conferring with classmates
- To spend more time reconsidering and improving their work
- To be more creative, to feel more confident, to be more productive

Johnson's list may be an ideal version of possibilities, but students are much more apt to take an active part in learning when they see themselves as part of the evaluation process.

Portfolios are commonly thought of as a collection of student writing and are most often used in English classes. But portfolios can include examples of drawings, problems, pictures of projects, audio- and videotapes, or whatever represents students' work. Also, portfolios are useful in every classroom. Several recent publications point out the usefulness of portfolios in math.

Evaluation in math class needs to be based on much more than exams. The California assessment committee for mathematics, as reported in *Portfolio News* (Fall 1990), offers several suggestions for student work that might be included in a portfolio. Selections from their list follow:

- Written descriptions of the results of practical or mathematical investigations
- Extended analyses of problem situations and investigation
- Descriptions and diagrams of problem-solving processes
- Statistical studies and graphic representations
- Group reports and photographs of student projects
- Excerpts from a student's math journal
- Self-report about what was learned

The report also lists advantages of portfolios.

- Evidence of performance beyond factual knowledge
- A clear and understandable picture, instead of a mysterious test score
- Opportunities for improved student self-image as a result of showing accomplishments rather than deficiencies
- Recognition of different learning styles, making assessment less culture-dependent and less biased
- An active role for students in assessing and selecting their work

Cristi Carson echoes the importance of portfolios in math by reporting on the experience of Nanette Seago, a math teacher. Seago believes the uniqueness of each student's portfolio "makes them a power tool, providing teachers with opportunities to learn what students know about content areas, to assess curriculum needs, and to become cognizant of how students are actually thinking (Carson, 1991, p. 6).

The Vermont Department of Education prepared brochures for students to use in preparing their math portfolios. "A Different Way of Looking at Math" is reproduced in *Portfolio News* (Fall 1991), and the portion on "Why Keep Math Portfolios?" follows:

> Looking at a collection of your work is a good way for you, your teacher(s), your parents, and others to see how you are doing in math. A portfolio contains problems and projects that you've really had a chance to work on. You'll have pieces from different times throughout the year so that you can see your progress over time. Looking at your solutions for complex problems tells more than just seeing answers on a test. A test answer only shows whether you were right or wrong. A portfolio piece

shows what you know and what you think, strategies or ways you solve problems, and how well you can explain these things. (p. 3)

An important aspect of portfolios is the opportunity for students to reflect on their work. Teachers accomplish this by having students write a letter to themselves reflecting on what they have learned as evidenced by the work in their portfolio and what they need or want to work on in the coming weeks. Some of the material in the portfolios is selected by teachers, some by students. Teachers provide guidelines for the selections. For example, I have requested the following pieces:

1. A level 3 piece including all of the discovery activities, drafts, revisions, and response sheets
2. An example of what you worked the hardest on
3. An example of what you learned the most from
4. The assignment you enjoyed doing the most
5. Anything of your own choosing (be sure to explain why you chose it)

All of the papers are dated to document progress and growth. Looking at day-to-day work often makes it difficult to see how much one has learned, and we all need reinforcement that shows we have improved. For students who are not making progress, the concrete evidence makes that obvious and can serve as motivation, especially when they reflect in their letter about how they plan on improving.

Portfolios encourage students to reflect about their work, from the standpoint of both what they have achieved and how they want to improve. Following are a few examples from my students' portfolios.

Dear Reader,

Welcome to my English Portfolio! It is a collection of my work throughout this past semester. I have included my memory story as the work that has been graded and revised. I chose this piece because it was a story that I spent a lot of time on and put a lot of effort into. Due to grammatical errors, I didn't get the grade that I would have liked so I chose this as my piece to revise.

This student, Christa, chose other pieces because "it was a creative idea," a section from a midterm because she "enjoyed the poetry," another because she "really had fun writing this story," another because "it was a fun project to do, and I was very pleased with the way it turned out." Of the nine selections in her portfolio, three were not graded, two were level 3, three were level 2, and one was level 1.

Denise, as part of the explanation for her choices, wrote:

I choose to include "Bruce the Talking Spruce" as my revised piece because it is representative of my childhood. As a free choice, I picked my poem "Violets" because it reveals my sentimental side. I always picked some for my mom when I was small. Both represent good childhood memories.

Heather chose a story that she felt was creative. "I'm usually *not* that creative so I was proud that I could write a story like Herbert." In describing goals, Laura wrote:

First, I would like to increase my vocabulary so that I am not always searching for words to use. I think my writing would be more effective if I had a broader range of vocabulary to choose from. And second, I would like to expand my creativity. I am much better at writing accounts of something that has already happened. I lack in the area of coming up with my own story.

Jennifer explained her goals:

One of my big problems is working on final drafts of papers. I feel I am very good about sitting down to do a rough draft immediately; however, I tend to put the paper away for an extended amount of time. My problem is not that I believe my paper is perfect; I suppose it is just procrastination. To remedy this problem, I plan to give myself goals to get the paper done. I have always heard it is beneficial to get your assignment done early and then set it aside for a bit. I still believe this to be a good idea; however, I am going to give myself only one day in-between. This allows for more drafts if necessary and gets my assignments in on time!

These examples and others reported by a variety of teachers illustrate how portfolios provide opportunities for writers to become active participants in the evaluation process.

Another advantage of using portfolios is the parent connection. They are a tremendous aid at parent–teacher conferences because a teacher is talking from a child's own work and not discussing evaluation in abstract terms. Not all parents come to conferences, but the portfolios can be mailed home.

Ruth Mitchell has students carry their portfolios home, and parents complete a questionnaire that reflects what they think about their child's work. The success of this method might depend on where one teaches, but Mitchell reports positive responses from parents, not only at the time they view the portfolio but throughout the year because they are more in touch with what is going on in school (Mitchell, 1992, pp. 110–114).

Assessment

Assessment is a type of evaluation that has a different purpose from the types previously discussed. Davis, Scriven, and Thomas (1987) explain that evaluation can have two general purposes: formative and summative. Analytic scales are formative; that is, they point out strengths and weaknesses of an individual's writing. Formative evaluation is designed to improve writing directly. Summative evaluation is used for discovering the overall quality of writing (Davis, et al., 1987, pp. 3–4). Assessment is summative and is used for large-scale evaluation.

School districts use assessment to determine how much their students know compared to a standardized norm. The areas commonly assessed are math, reading, and writing; students take the tests midway through the elementary grades, middle school, and high school. Assessment provides information not on individual students, but on curriculum and methods of teaching. If school districts want to know if their curriculum needs to change, they turn to assessment for the information. They learn how their district compares to other schools of the same size across the country.

The test for writing can be direct or indirect. Direct assessment is evaluation of a writing sample; indirect assessment is objective and is essentially an editing test. An indirect objective test is a list of multiple-choice questions where students identify subject–verb agreement, pronoun agreement, and punctuation. Direct assessment of writing samples more closely reflects classroom teaching of writing and gives students an opportunity to show how they can organize, compose, argue, and use a variety of words and sentences. Many tests include both types because a student may identify writing errors but not be able to compose interesting and thoughtful writing. The reverse might be true as well. Direct assessment is evaluated by a method of holistic scoring.

Holistic Scoring

Holistic scoring provides an overall evaluation of a paper. The paper is read quickly, as a "whole," and the evaluator decides if the writing is competent. Writing used for holistic grading is usually completed in one class period, although some test situations allow for multiple drafts. Either way, the evaluator does not write any comments on the paper because the writer never sees the paper, and does not receive a grade, only a number. The number signifies to the student if the writing was judged competent and does not give any information about improving the writing because the writers do not know what their strengths or weaknesses were (Maxwell, 1993, p. 146).

When evaluators use holistic scoring, they spend about two minutes on each paper, using scoring guides to determine the competence of the writing. An even number of scores works best because then a paper clearly is judged competent or not. For instance, if the possible scores are 1, 2, 3, and 4, the bottom two are not competent and the top two are. With an odd number of possibilities, the middle number is confusing. With 1, 2, 3, 4, and 5, is number 3 competent or not? Evaluators tend to score near the center and the center number should be avoided. Holistic scoring demands quick, decisive judgments; using a middle number only confuses these judgments (Maxwell, 1993, p. 146).

Holistic evaluation uses scoring guides with which the readers become familiar before determining the grade. The criteria include using detail, examples, support for claims, and clear expression of ideas. Control of writing conventions is also considered, but papers receiving the highest number are not free from errors. Good writers tend to write longer papers, and the chance of errors is greater. Because the writing samples are written in a test situation and usually within a limited time frame, the quality of writing is not as high as it would be under normal writing situations. Even if students have the time to read their papers over, the stress is likely high and the writing looks more like level 2 than level 3 and should be evaluated as such.

Although holistic grading is most frequently used in large-scale assessment, on occasion classroom use is appropriate. A teacher may want to know, in general, how well the students write, or to check on methods of instruction. At the beginning of a school year, the teacher has the students write on a specific topic and repeats the procedure near the end of the semester or year. By comparing the two scores, a teacher gains a sense of how a program is working.

Summary

Evaluation needs to consistently reflect a teacher's expectations of student performance, and students must always be informed about the teacher's expectations. Levels of writing form the framework for evaluation. Purposes of the writing activities determine levels and, therefore determine the type of evaluation. Several types of evaluation are appropriate in the classroom. Informal evaluation that does not include a grade has an important part in helping students improve their writing. Student involvement in evaluation needs to occur for all types. Self-evaluation is the beginning of the evaluation process. Impression grading is used by teachers to get a quick review of students' work. Analytical grading scales are valuable tools for informing students about the reasons for the grade they receive. Large-scale assessment is used when a school district wants to know how its students compare to a national norm. When writing samples are used as part of the assessment, they are evaluated by holistic grading. Portfolios involve students in their own evaluation and provide a way for them to reflect on their progress.

Discussion Questions

1. How can evaluation actually help students improve their writing?
2. How does a teacher establish purpose for an assignment?
3. Why are all three levels important in teaching writing?

4. Discuss the advantages and disadvantages of informal grading.
5. How might self-evaluation improve your writing?
6. Discuss the advantages and disadvantages of analytical grading.
7. Discuss the implication of students' involvement in their evaluation.

Suggested Activities

1. Using an assignment you wrote for another class, write a critique of your paper's strong and weak points. List the areas you want to improve.
2. Develop a grading scale for the paper you used in activity 1 that fits the purpose as you understand it.
3. Design a writing assignment in your subject area for secondary students. Describe the purpose and establish a level.
4. Design a level 3 writing assignment for secondary students and develop an analytic grading scale. In small groups, compare what you wrote and critique one another's.
5. Create a portfolio from assignments you did for this class. Select one piece from which you learned the most, one with which you are the most satisfied, and one of your own choice. Write a paragraph explaining why you selected the ones you did. Write a second paragraph explaining your goals for your own writing.

References

Belanoff, Pat, & Marcia Dickson, eds. *Portfolios.* Portsmouth, NH: Boynton/Cook, 1991.

Carson, Cristi. "Why Math Portfolios." *Portfolio News,* Winter 1991, p. 6.

Davis, Barbara Gross, Michael Scriven, & Susan Thomas. *The Evaluation of Composition Instruction.* New York: Teachers College Press, 1987.

Elbow, Peter. *Embracing Contraries.* New York: Oxford University Press, 1987.

Elbow, Peter. *What Is English?* New York: Modern Language Association, 1990.

Herter, Roberta J. "Writing Portfolios: Alternative to Testing." *English Journal,* January 1991, pp. 90–92.

Johnson, Martha. "Wedding Process to Product and Assessment to Learning." *Portfolio News,* Spring 1991, p. 2.

Krest, Margie. "Adapting the Portfolio to Meet Student Needs." *English Journal,* February 1990, pp. 29–34.

"Math Portfolios" *Portfolio News,* Fall 1990, p. 11.

Maxwell, Rhoda, & Mary Meiser. *Teaching English in Middle and Secondary Schools.* New York: Macmillan, 1993.

Mitchell, Ruth. *Testing for Learning.* New York: Free Press, 1992.

Tierney, Robert, Mark A. Carter, & Laura E. Desal. *Portfolio Assessment in the Reading-Writing Classroom.* Norwood, MA: Christopher-Gordon, 1991.

Yancey, Kathleen Blake, ed. *Portfolios in the Classroom.* Urbana, IL: National Council of Teachers of English, 1992.

Vermont Department of Education. "Explaining Portfolios to Students in Vermont." *Portfolio News,* 3(1), Fall 1991, pp. 3+.

11

INTERDISCIPLINARY UNITS

We are coming to recognize that we cannot train people in specializations and expect them to cope with the multifaceted nature of their work. . . . The renewed trend in the schools toward interdisciplinary will help students better integrate strategies from their studies into the larger world.
—HEIDI HAYES JACOBS, 1989, P. 6

Prereading Questions

1. Define and describe what you believe to be a unit of study.
2. What disciplines are best suited to unit planning?
3. Describe what interdisciplinary units you studied in secondary school. What were the benefits and drawbacks for the students?
4. What problems might teachers have in planning units?
5. What are the major strengths in unit planning and teaching?

Introduction

Interdisciplinary units are becoming more and more a part of the curriculum. An interdisciplinary curriculum is based on the idea supported by cognitive psychologists that knowledge and skills are synergistic. Knowledge is increased and learning easier when interconnections are made rather than presenting lessons in isolation (Amdur, 1993, p. 12). When connections are made among disciplines, motivation and application are a natural outcome; also, learning is more accessible to a wider variety of learning styles and abilities.

Rationale for Interdisciplinary Teaching

Course content is often a stumbling block for high school teachers when they consider an integrated model. They are concerned that the information and knowledge inherent in their subject matter will not be covered adequately in a multi-content approach. However, an interdisciplinary unit "more accurately represents the application of knowledge to life in a complex society" (Dybdahl & Shaw, 1993, p. 38). We need to consider many points of view when learning about a subject and when making decisions. Through integrated curriculum, students learn about varying perspectives as they are "compared, contrasted, and encouraged" (p. 38). Units are effective at the secondary level because students are allowed to pursue topics that concern and interest them while also learning the course content mandated by curriculum.

Adolescents have concerns about self-concept and their relationships with others. They have questions about the world around them: "the environment, wealth and poverty, war and peace, cultural diversity and interdependence" (Coppage, 1994, p. 32). Stephen Tchudi points out that:

> The thrust of interdisciplinary, language-based education is toward bridging that school/other-world gap, principally by showing students that "real" or "hard knowledge," constructed by the learner, grows from experience and gives the individual a degree of control over the world. (Tchudi, 1993, p. xiv)

These concerns are best presented through a multidimensional approach involving several disciplines, where information and knowledge from several sources come together in a common focus.

A unit that illustrates how real-world problems, students' interest, and curriculum goals can all be included is one designed by Jim Burke, a high school English teacher. Burke chose social problems as a unit but then had the students generate a list of social problems from which students made individual choices. He gave them an overview of his expectations and a rubric of the project plan. The class was organized into a workshop format requiring students to work both independently and in groups. They were required to read two articles that dealt with their topic and hand in summaries of the articles. Other curriculum goals that were met included a level 3 report and public speaking when they presented their papers to the class.

As the project developed the students found they needed to "communicate with real people in their community" (Burke, 1993, p. 16). Writing interviews and surveys became necessary. First, though, they studied sample interviews and questionnaires and discussed how to write ones that helped them acquire the information they needed without biases or slanted answers. Through their involvement with the community, they learned how to interact with people in a variety of situations.

Students learned that while they cannot solve vast problems, there are some actions they can take to alleviate them. Their increased sense of civic involvement led them to write letters to local and national politicians and helped them to gain a sense of empowerment. The result was that students did their best work about a problem they came to care about. Burke hopes they will carry this sense of social obligation with them throughout their lives.

A major challenge for teachers today is the amount of information available. Teachers need to accept the reality that it is impossible to know all the facts and that they cannot teach all there is to know about any subject to their students. However, teachers can help students know how to form concepts, make generalizations based on facts, and develop "conceptual understanding of themselves in relation to the world in which they live" (McGuire & Noe, 1993, p. 2). It is important for students to understand the relationships among different disciplines and to see the applications of what they learn to the wider world.

Organizing teaching around units increases students' interest and motivation because the unit themes can center on issues important to their lives. Students discover connections among the topics from several contents, certainly a more realistic view of how the world works. Also, the units provide the "why" of what they are learning because the learning fits into a broader context than when studying content information separately. It is important for teachers to accept students' effort and interest in the learning process even when they obviously have a less well developed and less mature sense of the content. Connecting subject-matter information with the students' knowledge and experience is vital for effective learning, and this happens more easily in an integrated curriculum. Young people do not categorize knowledge along disciplinary lines (McGuire & Noe, 1993, p. 1). This artificial way of dividing up knowledge happens only in school.

Units are apt to take on a life of their own. Once students become involved in a topic, they tend to carry the ideas further than the teachers originally planned. Interdisciplinary units need to provide many opportunities for exploration, talking, and listening, regardless of the subject. Without these connections, students are not likely to see how skills and knowledge obtained in one subject can transfer to another. Students who cannot see connections across content are "unlikely to be able to use their knowledge and skills to solve problems or make decisions about issues raised in the curriculum (Lipson, Valencia, Wixson, & Peters, 1993, p. 253). Interdisciplinary courses and projects help students see the relationships and contributions of different disciplines, thus providing for a wide variety of student interests, abilities, and viewpoints (Chuska, 1989, p. 36). Such an arrangement helps break down the isolation of subject matter and allows for a more in-depth study using varied resources (p. 46). As students explore divergent points of view and pursue individual interests, they become more capable independent learners.

In content areas, textbooks are often the only reading material students use. For many students, the textbooks are difficult to read; these students do not acquire much knowledge from them. Also, using only a textbook does not allow for in-depth study of topics of special interest to individual students (Smith & Johnson, 1993, p. 54). Designing an interdisciplinary unit brings together reading material from a variety of sources that extends the textbook information and allows students to follow up on individual interests that relate to the topic being studied. Successful units include a variety of reading and writing activities as well as many opportunities for discussion, working with peers, and contacting people and places outside of the classroom. In general, interdisciplinary units help students and teachers connect learning with the real world.

An example of a unit that demonstrates how effective units can connect with the real world is one on an environmental issue designed by Jackie Williams and Terry Deal Reynolds for a middle school classroom. Four subject areas—science, social studies, language arts, and math—were included in the unit, but the teaching was not differentiated among the subject areas. In science, the activities centered on river pollution and wastewater discharge from paper mills. From social studies, the activities centered on the political, economic, and social implications of the issue. Students came to realize that there are many sides to an issue. In this case, jobs and livelihoods had to balance with the environment and natural resources. Language arts focused on readings related to the issues, interviews, vocabulary, note-taking, and oral presentations. Math skills were applied during the stream sampling because students had to manipulate the data they collected and then apply mathematical formulas. "By the end of the unit, the students knew more about this local controversy than many of their well-informed parents and teachers" (Williams & Reynolds, 1993, p. 14).

Planning Interdisciplinary Curricula

Planning for units of study takes thought, time, and commitment. Units developed without careful consideration of educational objectives do not constitute sound curriculum. Dennis Coppage (1994) explains that even if a unit includes social studies, math, and other content areas, "subject areas without development of important ideas constitute correlation, not true integrations" (Coppage, 1994, p. 31). Planners need to begin by identifying "big understandings" that have broad learner objectives relevant to students' lives.

Planners need to consider a balance in content-related goals. If a social studies teacher is planning a unit on the westward movement and asks the music teacher to come in and teach a song from that era, the goals are only for social studies. The song might be interesting and entertaining for students but would not by itself teach any music curriculum. In fact, this type of planning disrupts the coherence of the curriculum. Effective integration accomplishes "significant curricular goals in two or more subjects" (Alleman & Brophy, 287). Careful planning among teachers is needed to ensure that appropriate content is taught.

Heidi Hayes Jacobs, a well-known authority on designing interdisciplinary curriculum, writes that the "idea is to bring together discipline perspectives and focus them on the investigation of a target theme, issue, or problem" (Jacobs, 1989,

p. 54). The topic must be relevant to the students. Teachers provide a sequence for the unit and the reasons for teaching a topic (p. 59). Jacobs explains:

> No matter what the content, we can design active linkages between fields of knowledge. We can teach the works of Shakespeare with an eye to the history of the times, the arts, the values, the role of science, and the zeitgeist rather than simply sticking with specific passages. . . . The curriculum becomes more relevant when there are connections between subjects rather than strict isolation. (Jacobs, 1989, p. 5)

Williams and Reynolds (1993) suggest that the best way to integrate the curriculum is for all of the subject-area teachers together to develop thematic units (p. 15). That way, each teacher has responsibility for the success of the unit and develops a sense of ownership.

Depending on the age and interests of students, teachers can choose an issue such as justice, freedom, or peace. The issue is broad, and the project is organized from brainstorming topics generated by teachers and their students (Baska, 1994, p. 57). Another way of organizing a unit is to make a list from an existing topic, such as the environment, and have students and teachers together decide what aspects to explore. The concept they choose is the unit for exploration. A unit is an elaborated plan that begins broadly and then is defined by questions and areas of instruction (Baska, 1994, p. 91). A unit must be flexible so that students can always have input into the planning. If all the lessons are predetermined, the unit does not allow opportunities for topics to arise from the study or for learning in which the students are involved.

A group of music educators (Kite, Smucker, Steiner, & Bayne, 1994) found that when developing interdisciplinary curriculum, they were "better able to integrate effectively across subject areas by looking beyond our respective disciplines" (p. 35). They were most successful when using a thematic approach for teaching content. Incorporating effective music listening into general education was the basis for their integrated methods courses. They emphasize that, when implementing an interdisciplinary teaching model inclusive of the arts, music or the arts should not become a sideline but should remain a central focus (p. 36).

Team teaching is an effective way of organizing a unit because teachers bring their own knowledge and interests to the planning. Teams are generally made up of teachers representing English, social studies, math, and science, although some schools may have a different configuration. Many middle schools are organized around teams where four teachers are responsible for a team equivalent to four classrooms. The groups of students are not static and can be formed in the way that best suits the current teaching situation. Such a fluid organization makes team planning and unit teaching natural and efficient.

However, this type of situation is not required for a group of teachers to work well together. What is necessary is the willingness to listen to each other and to believe in the validity of collaborative teaching. Kim O'Day, an eighth-grade teacher, writes that "just as we emphasize collaborative learning today, we should embrace collaborative teaching" (O'Day, 1994, p. 40). For team teaching to be successful, the teachers need to be competent in their fields. They need to share the big goals as well as the details of the unit, such as grading, class rules, and all the factors that go into running a class.

Units do not look alike. Some are planned by a team of teachers who jointly teach the unit; others by one teacher who incorporates other curricular areas in his or her classroom; and some by teachers who plan the unit together but teach parts in their own content classes. Examples of six units designed in all three of these ways are described next.

Tracing One's Roots

A teacher, Rebecca Olien, designed a unit to include English, social studies, art, and music to create a rich tapestry of experiences as students explore their past. The unit begins with a discussion of ancestors. What does it mean to say one has "ancestors" or an "ethnic background"? After the introductory activities, students fill out a questionnaire about their background during class time. Here is a sample of questions:

> Where did your ancestors come from?
> When did they come to this country and why?
> What were their ages when they came?
> What was life like for them?
> Did they have jobs?
> Were they married?
> Did they travel alone?

Generally, students discover they know remarkably little about these people, unless their families have immigrated recently. Students take the questionnaire home and, with the help of relatives, fill out the information as completely as possible. Then students share the information in class through discussion. The locations of their ancestors' homelands are identified on a world map displayed in the classroom.

For the next activity, students choose someone to interview about their family background. This person is usually a family member, but it does not have to be. A Native American student may wish to interview a tribal leader, or a student may want to interview a person who knows a great deal about a particular group. Students write the interview questions and work on them in revision groups. Once the interview (by phone, mail, or in person) is completed, students write a report based on all the information they have accumulated. In addition to the questionnaire and interview, they may read journal articles and books depending on their own ability and level.

While they are collecting information and writing the report, students are also reading historical fiction and discussing their books in response groups. Class discussion centers on what makes historical fiction interesting. How much factual information is included? Once the reports are completed, the students write a fiction story based on their information.

The culminating activity is a "cultural week." Students work in groups to create a presentation to the class on a particular culture. Many students have several cultures in their background and they may select whichever one they wish for the presentation. Also, students may wish to group cultures of similar backgrounds into one presentation. The presentation focuses on the music, art, crafts, and food of the countries. Students bring samples of food and artifacts to help illustrate their ancestral background. Many teach a few words of their language and dress in traditional costume.

The unit is designed to not only help students learn more about their background but also to develop pride in their ancestors and an awareness of the richness of other people's cultural background (from Maxwell & Meiser, 1993, pp. 330–331).

Analyzing Household Products

Olien's unit, described earlier, took place in one classroom. A group of middle school teachers designed a unit where each teacher was responsible for the part associated with a particular content; however, the teachers planned the unit together. The unit begins in science class with discussion of which household products are the most effective. The students bring in varieties of toothpaste, cleanser, detergent, and other common household products. The science teacher assists them in setting up experiments to test for foaming action, pH, viscosity, abrasion, and other characteristics associated with each product. The students work in groups conducting experiments and keeping careful detailed notes.

The next step is a social studies activity. The students write a survey to collect opinions on the products: taste, smell, feel, and appearance. First, they discuss who uses surveys and for what purposes. Students write the questions for the survey so that the desired data will be collected, which takes preplanning and thought. They also learn the importance of a population sample and of targeting the appropriate group to survey. In math class, when the data from the surveys are in, students learn how to construct graphs and charts to visualize the results. Also in math the students work on which product is the most cost-effective and make a chart to show the results.

Students bring the notes from science, social studies, and math to English class. Here they use computers to write a report explaining their tests and the results. Because they are using word processing to produce the report, they learn how to adjust tabs, use boldface type, and set margins. Writing conclusions to the report takes careful planning to reflect all that they have learned.

The culminating activity is writing advertisements for the products they worked on. The English teacher leads students in a discussion of how the data they collected could be used in advertising the product. How might advertising agencies play down unfavorable attributes and highlight the positive? How might results be manipulated? How can *not* saying something help to sell products? What techniques are used commonly in the media to convince people to buy a particular product? Students work in groups to write an advertisement and then produce it for television. The art teacher helps students with graphic design; the music teacher helps them write jingles. After revision and practice, the ads are taped and later shown to all the students. Betsy Damon, the English teacher, said the students' enthusiasm and learning makes the extra planning time well worthwhile, and the teachers continue the unit each year.

Columbus's Voyages

Interest in one topic can provide the framework for increased understanding and interest in related topics. An example of a unit that illustrates this is one on Christopher Columbus's voyages designed by Joseph Enedy, Tony Graham, and Paul Cline (1994). They selected several disciplines to show relationships with the necessary knowledge to carry out the voyages.

- *Science and math:* Knowledge of astronomy was essential to the explorers. The compass and astrolabe were extremely important.
- *Government:* The monarchy of Spain, the feudal system, issues of war and peace, and international relationships all had a bearing on Columbus's situation and outcome.
- *Economics:* Columbus's major goal in the voyages was to find gold and spices. Instead, he found tobacco and many new foods.
- *History:* Many myths surround Columbus as a personality and an explorer. His reasons for making the trips, the knowledge of the times, and the kind of man he was have many different interpretations.
- *Religion:* Columbus intended to spread Christianity to any new lands he discovered and believed in the right to proclaim sovereignty over "heathen and infidel" domains.
- *Geography:* Knowledge of the world area was limited during the 1400s, yet Columbus had somewhat of a world view because of his vast experience as a sailor.

Combining these disciplines into a coherent study helps students to understand the era of Columbus and to gain perspective on his voyages. The authors suggest several activities that encompass various content areas. Students could create an astrolabe, compass, maps, globes, and ship models. An extended study of maps illustrates past misconceptions and today's increased knowledge. Students could examine the type of data Columbus used to determine the distance from Spain to China, and then do their own calculations. The topic is rich in possibilities for interdisciplinary instruction (Euedy et al., 1994, pp. 149–151).

Preserving the Rain Forests

A study of rain forests is usually associated only with science and social studies. Marcia Rosenbusch, however, suggests teaching a rain forest theme in the foreign language classroom. Rosenbusch designed this unit for elementary level, and I adapted it for secondary students.

Social studies prepares students to be responsible citizens. That objective is broadened to prepare them to be responsible world citizens. The responsibilities of global citizens include helping to solve world problems, understand and care for others, protect and use natural resources wisely, and promote an attitude of peaceful cooperation (Rosenbusch, 1994, p. 31). Themes that come from content areas addressing these responsibilities might include poverty, pollution, energy, and the use of natural resources. Rosenbusch used the theme of natural resources to develop a unit on Costa Rican rain forests in Spanish classes. The unit was planned around four main areas: knowledge, skills, values, and social participation.

Knowledge about Costa Rica and rain forests came from books, articles, films, videotapes, and personal experiences. Students learn about many facets pertaining to the unit:

- Identify and describe typical plants, animals, and birds of the Costa Rican rain forest.
- Identify the general characteristics of a rain forest.
- Compare the physical features, climate, and plant and animal life of their own environment to that of the Costa Rican rain forest.
- Learn about food products.
- Learn about the threats to the existence of rain forests.
- Describe ways that people are working to preserve rain forests.

Teachers from social studies, foreign language, and language arts work together to accomplish these goals.

Skills are developed from the knowledge base the students acquire. For instance, after they learn about the levels of the rain forest, they can apply this information in hypothesizing differences in the microclimate at the emergent level and the floor level for the amount of sunlight, rainfall, and wind. After learning about the destruction of the rain forests, students write about the future for the life forms of the rain forest if the destruction continues and their suppositions about the continued destruction. The material used is in Spanish, so the enhancement of Spanish language skills is improved throughout the unit.

Values are taught by examining differing values and points of view—for example, the views of those who want to make a living from the rain forest and of those who want to preserve it. The teacher does not present the problem as one of bad versus good but encourages students to look at the issue from all sides.

Social participation is encouraged by providing opportunities for action to increase their understanding. Students can research all viewpoints on issues and formulate their own ideas on how to solve a global problem.

Several art activities enhance learning throughout the unit. Rosenbusch describes one activity in which students construct a Morpho butterfly. Photographs of the butterfly are placed around the classroom as visual aids in creating this beautiful blue creature. Through the physical activity of designing the butterfly, students learn in detail the characteristics of the Morpho butterfly.

By combining social studies, foreign language, art, and language arts in this thematic unit, the students' perception of themselves as global citizens increases through knowledge and awareness.

Prehistoric Cultures

This unit, designed by David Amdur (1993), is integrated across the disciplines of social studies, visual art, studio art, and literature. These separate humanities courses enrich each other by the wealth of material from all the subject areas. The classes are taught separately; the integration occurs by coordinating the subject material to parallel and enforce one another.

The social studies teacher introduces the unit with a documentary film on the Waldanni tribe in the Amazon jungle. The film portrays a small egalitarian hunting band that exhibits strength, skill, and ingenuity. The English teacher has students read literature that reflects the tribe's respect for the natural world, for example Chief Seattle's letter. Students discuss the relation between this text's values and the ones evident in the social studies film. The social studies teacher introduces the related spiritual beliefs of animism and shamanism.

The visual arts class examines reproductions of Paleolithic cave painting thought to be products of shamanistic initiation rituals. In a related studio exercise, students create random patterns by spilling ink on sheets of paper, and then search these patterns for a suggestion of a latent image. Students enhance the images by the application of translucent layers of acrylic paint. Following this, they exchange the paintings and write brief descriptions of what they see in each other's work. They discuss the relation between form and imagination based on the images they created.

The social studies class explores the differences in Neolithic and Paleolithic cultures. In visual art class, students study the transformation from naturalistic to abstract imagery. In studio art, students draw naturalistic figures and then progressively create a series of more abstract drawings. Through a study of prehistoric cultures, students gain broad understanding of the differences between two fundamentally different cultures and the concept of naturalism, as well as the connections between cultures, values, and art.

Science and Society

Team teaching is an excellent way to break down the barriers dividing disciplines and to provide teachers with opportunities to learn from one another. A group of high school teachers designed a team-taught course that includes science, social studies, and English (Carvellas, Blanchette, & Parren, 1993).

Because high school students will soon be making decisions in an increasingly technological society, these teachers designed a course, "Science and Society," to help students in several ways:

1. Become skillful at obtaining factual information from a variety of sources reflecting multiple points of view by writing annotated bibliographies.
2. Make informed decisions based on their findings by writing position papers after they learn to recognize bias, distinguish fact from opinion, and use statistics.
3. Act on their beliefs by writing letters to elected representatives and to newspapers, holding debates for the public, and producing slide shows, among other activities.
4. Formulate personal philosophies that are applied consistently across issues by developing statements of belief as part of their take-home exam. (p. 86)

To begin the unit, teachers assign articles on topics to teams of students who present summaries and critical reviews to the class. When the presentations are completed, students brainstorm on additional topics they could study that relate to science, technology, and society. Teachers also suggest topics that may not occur to students. The class draws up a comprehensive list, students rank their top five choices, and the topics are chosen for the year.

Students are encouraged to use a wide range of resources, including interviews, invited speakers, articles, congressional records, Newsbank, and other library sources. Students tend to believe what they hear from authorities or read in print, but over the year they come to recognize biases and seek opposing points of view. Oral presentations and class presentations help students think through their positions and help teachers to evaluate students' progress.

To help students become responsible citizens, teachers emphasize that forming an opinion is not enough; they must take action to effect change. Students invite professionals to their class to discuss issues with them. They write plays to present information to elementary school grades, coordinate panel discussions for the community, testify before state legislative committees, distribute flyers, present at state conferences, and hold symposiums.

Power of the Media

A history and English teacher, Kristi Bothe, designed the following unit to teach in both her content areas at the eighth-grade level. She choose this particular theme because of the interest middle school students have in the media and the importance in helping them to understand the complexities of media influence and the potential problems with censorship. Bothe identifies the level of writing for each writing activity.

Part 1

Before the students listen to the broadcast of *The War of the Worlds,* it is important for them to understand what was happening in 1938. She assigns the students to groups of five and assigns each group a topic covering aspects of the historic period. Students must answer the following questions regarding their topic: who, what, where, why, and how. Students take notes while working in groups (level 1). The five topics are domestic politics, foreign politics, music, economics, and technology. Each group becomes an expert on the assigned topic and is responsible for teaching the information to the rest of the class so that all students have the necessary background for the time period. The students write a short paper based on their topic (level 2).

The students select a science book to read and respond in their journal as they read (level 1). While they are reading, time is set aside for discussion of their books.

Students listen to the broadcast of *War of the Worlds* in class. Bothe periodically stops the tape for discussion, and students are expected to take notes (level 1). In addition, she directs their responses by asking them to think about the following issues:

- What in particular do you notice about the events that are occurring?
- What aspects of the broadcast could make listeners believe it was real?
- If you were listening to this broadcast live in 1938, what might you be thinking?

Also, Bothe encourages students to draw pictures depicting the invasion, the aliens, scenes as described by the narrative, or the aftermath. Students write whether they believe the broadcast of this story was ethical (level 2).

Resources for the first section:

Allen, Frederick Lewis. *Since Yesterday: The Nineteen Thirties in America—September 3, 1929–September 3, 1939.* Harper & Row, 1986.
American Heritage Illustrated History of the United States. Vol. 14: *The Roosevelt Era.* Choice, 1988.
Carter, Alden. *Radio from Marconi to The Space Age.* Watts, 1987.

Editor of Time–Life Books. *This Fabulous Century.* Vol. 4: *1930–1949.* Time–Life, 1969.
Shannon, David A. *Between the Wars: America, 1919 to 1941.* Houghton, 1979.
Welles, Orson. *The War of the Worlds.* Original radio broadcast, October 31, 1938. Recording.

Examples of science fiction, but students may select their own:

Bunting, Eve. *Strange Things Happen in the Woods.*
Cobett, Scott. *Deadly Hoax.*
Faville, Barry. *The Return.*
Foster, John. *Spaceways: An Anthology of Space Poems.*
Hoover, H. M. *The Shepherd Moon.*
Key, Alexander. *The Forgotten Door.*
Service, Pamela. *Earthseed.*

Part 2

During class, students look at newspaper clippings about the broadcast. They discuss how newspapers have changed over the last fifty years. Students write a short paper comparing these newspapers with the present (level 2). Next, students work in groups again to write a radio drama. Bothe teaches them how to write a script. Students incorporate sound effects and music into the script. Each group records the drama for the class to listen to. As the writing groups are in progress, Bothe arranges for a visit to the audiovisual center. The students write three questions they want answered before taking the tour. The tour gives them ideas on how to incorporate the use of the equipment into their scripts.

The discussions of the science fiction books they are reading continues throughout this period.

Sources for Part 2:

Balcyiak, Bill. *Radio* Florida: Rouke Enterprises, 1989.
Duke, Charles R. *Creative Dramatics and English Teaching.* Urbana, IL: National Council of Teachers of English, 1974.
McCaslin, Nellie. *Creative Drama in the Intermediate Grades: A Handbook for Teachers.* New York: Longman, 1987.
McLeish, Robert. *The Technique of Radio Production.* New York: Focal Press, 1989.
Nisbett, Alec. *The Techniques of Sound (Sound Effects).* New York: Focal Press, 1989.

Part 3

This part begins with time for class discussion on the science fiction books students are reading. In groups, the students share their ideas about alien life and the power of the media in regard to aliens. Recent TV shows that deal with this topic are shown and discussed. Following a class discussion of how aliens are portrayed in the books they are reading, they write a short paper about the similarities and differences of the aliens (level 2). Additionally, the class discusses poems about aliens using the Foster anthology. Students then write a poem about aliens (level 1).

The students watch a taped news broadcast that highlights a current concern or interest, such as "20/20," "Dateline," or "48 Hours." They then discuss the freedom of the press and the influence of the news shows. In journals, students write about how believable the show is and what ethical issues may be involved (level 1).

Class time is provided for groups to continue working on the scripts.

Sources for Part 3:

Altheide, David. *Media Power.*
Bernards, Ned. *Mass Media.*
Evans, J. Edward. *Freedom of the Press.*
Seldes, Gilbert. *The New Mass Media: Challenge to a Free Society.*
Terkel, Susan Neilburg. *Ethics.*

Part 4

Students finish up their scripts and then tape the program using the audiovisual equipment. They write a brief paper describing what they learned from working on this project (level 2). The tapes are presented in class.

The next topic is censorship, and students begin by writing a definition, what types might exist, and reasons for censorship in their journals (level 1). During class discussion, Bothe raises questions concerning present-day censorship.

- Are there shows on TV or radio that you think should be censored? If so, why?
- Who should decide if something is banned?

Children's books that have been banned over the last twenty years are discussed and the basis for censorship determined. Students write a letter to a fictitious school board assuming the role of a parent who wishes a book to be removed from the school (level 2). Students then meet in groups and assume the role of school board members who have received the letters. As a group, they debate whether or not the book(s) need to be censored and reach a consensus. They write a letter to the parents supporting the view they support (level 2).

The final activity of the unit is a debate. The class is divided in half and each side takes an opposing view to the following statement:

The media are accurate and factual; therefore, citizens should not censor or question the ethics of the media.

Students can use any materials from the unit in preparing their arguments.

Sources for part 4:

Bellairs, John. *House with a Clock in Its Walls.*
Brindze, Ruth. *Not to Be Broadcast: The Truth about Radio.*
Byars, Betsy. *Cracker Jackson.*
Collier, James. *My Brother Sam Is Dead.*
Creswick, Paul. *Robin Hood.*
George, Jean Craighead. *Julie of the Wolves.*
Hahn, Mary Downing. *Wait Till Helen Comes.*
L'Engle, Madeleine. *A Wrinkle in Time.*
Melody, William H. *Children's Television: The Economics of Exploitation.*
Paterson, Katherine. *Bridge to Terabithia.*
Prelutsky, Jack. *Nightmares to Trouble Your Sleep.*
Schwartz, Alvin. *Scary Stories 3.*
Snyder, Zilpha Keatley. *Witches of Worm.*
Television and Values. Film. The Learning Seed Company.
Twain, Mark. *Huckleberry Finn.*
Viorst, Judith. *Alexander and the Terrible, Horrible, No Good, Very Bad Day.*
Wilder, Laura Ingalls. *Little House on the Prairie.*

Representations of History through the Arts

The final unit described here combines art and history. The unit was designed by Terrie Epstein (1994) for eleventh-graders. The theme is late-nineteenth-century European and Asian immigration to the United States. Students begin by reading the section on immigration in their textbooks. From then on, all the resources are primary sources. They discuss oral histories, view photographs of immigrants, and interpret nineteenth-century poems and cartoons by and about immigrants. The study is framed by two broad questions: How did immigrants interpret their experiences as immigrants? How did reformers and nativists portray the immigrant experience? As a final activity, students represent something they have learned by creating a story, poem, painting, collage, song, or other work of art. By representing history through these art forms, students communicate the texture of actual human experience (Epstein, 1994, p. 136). Epstein's students showed a strong understanding of the immigrant experience through the blending of art and history.

Summary

Integrated curriculum more accurately represents our complicated society. Units bring together disciplines to examine topics relevant to students' lives. Studies across curriculum help students recognize and appreciate many points of view. Units are effective because students pursue topics in depth and acquire real-world knowledge. It is important for students to understand the relationships among disciplines and to understand the applications of their learning to the wider world.

The examples described here are meant to be ideas and suggestions to help new teachers start on their own planning and organizing. Although some types of unit design are not feasible in some schools, there always are ways to extend teaching and learning beyond the confines of a particular subject. Both teachers and students benefit.

Discussion Questions

1. What are the inherent problems or dangers in designing interdisciplinary units?
2. What are the advantages of interdisciplinary units?
3. What topics not covered in the chapter lend themselves to an interdisciplinary approach?
4. What are the first steps in planning an interdisciplinary unit?
5. How might you convince a teacher who never has used units to agree to work with you on developing one?

Suggested Activities

1. Beginning with the content area you will teach, decide on a topic for a thematic unit appropriate for the students' level and your interests. Share your idea with the class, and through discussion form small groups based on similar interests. Each group then develops a unit.
2. Design a unit that you would teach by yourself, and include related content goals.
3. Form groups of four students representing different content areas. Choose an abstract topic, like truth, beauty, or honor, and plan a unit that includes curricular goals from all your subject areas.
4. Write a letter to the school board convincing them to reorganize the schedule so that team teaching is a possibility.
5. Choose two content areas that seem to have no connections and design a unit that encompasses both. Examples might include science and physical education, or math and art, or a foreign language and health.

References

Alleman, Janet, & Jere Brophy. "Is Curriculum Integration a Boon or a Threat to Social Studies?" *Social Education, 57*(6), 1993, pp. 287–291.

Amdur, David. "Arts and Culture Context." *Art Education,* May 1993, pp. 12–19.

Baska, Joyce Van Tassel. *Comprehensive Curriculum for Gifted Learners,* 2nd ed. Boston: Allyn and Bacon, 1994.

Bothe, Kristi. "Power of Media." Unpublished manuscript, December 1994.

Brandt, Ron. "On Interdisciplinary Curriculum: A Conversation with Heidi Hayes Jacobs." *Educational Leadership,* October 1991, pp. 24–26.

Burke, Jim. "Tackling Society's Problems in English Class." *Educational Leadership,* April 1993, pp. 16–18.

Carvellas, Betty, Brad Blanchette, & Lauren Parren. "Science and Society: Escape to the Real World." In Stephen Tchudi, ed., *The Astonishing Curriculum* (pp. 85–91). Urbana, IL: National Council of Teachers of English, 1993.

Chuska, Kenneth R. *Gifted Learners.* Bloomington, IN: National Educational Service, 1989.

Cook, Gillian E., & Marian L. Martinello. "Topics and Themes in Interdisciplinary Curriculum." *Middle School Journal,* January 1994, pp. 40–44.

Coppage, Dennis. "Forming Collaborative Partnerships: Social Studies, Language Arts and Reading Teachers Interact." *WSRA Journal,* Winter 1994, pp. 31–33.

Dybdahl, Claudia S., & Donna Gail Shaw. "It's More Than Reading a Book." *Science Activities,* Summer 1993, pp. 34–39.

Enedy, Joseph D., Tony Graham, & Paul C. Cline. "An Interdisciplinary Approach to Teaching Christopher Columbus." *Social Education, 58*(3), 1994, pp. 149–151.

Epstein, Terrie L. "Sometimes a Shining Moment: High School Students' Representations of History through the Arts." *Social Education, 58*(3), pp. 1994. 136–141.

Henquinet, Amy. "Thematic Teaching Unit—Heroes" Unpublished manuscript, May 1994, pp. 1–11.

Jacobs, Heidi Hayes, ed. *Interdisciplinary Curriculum: Design and Implementation.* Alexandria, VA: Association for Supervision and Curriculum Development, 1989.

Kite, Thomas S., Thomas Smucker, Stan Steiner, & Mina Bayne. "Using Program Music for Interdisciplinary Study." *Music Educators Journal,* March 1994, pp. 33–36+.

Lipson, Marjorie Y., Sheila W. Valencia, Karen K. Wixson, & Charles W. Peters. "Integration and Thematic Teaching: Integration to Improve Teaching and Learning." *Language Arts, 70,* 1993, pp. 252–263.

Maxwell, Rhoda, & Mary Meiser. *Teaching English in Middle and Secondary Schools.* New York: Macmillan, 1993.

McGuire, M. E., & K. S. Noe. "Natural Partners: Using Reading and Writing to Promote Social Studies Understanding." *International Journal of Social Education,* Autumn 1993, pp. 1–11.

O'Day, Kim. "Using Formal and Informal Writing in Middle School Social Studies." *Social Education,* January 1994, pp. 39–40.

Rosenbusch, Marcia H. "Preserve the Rain Forests." *The Social Studies,* January/February 1994, pp. 31–35.

Routman, Regie. *Invitations.* Portsmouth, NH: Heinemann, 1991.

Smith, Lea J., & Holly Johnson. "Interdisciplinary Thematic Literature Studies." *Language Arts Journal of Michigan, 8*(2), 1993, pp. 54–67.

Tchudi, Stephen, ed. *The Astonishing Curriculum.* Urbana, IL: National Council of Teachers of English, 1993.

Williams, Jackie, & Terry Deal Reynolds. "Courting Controversy: How to Build Interdisciplinary Units." *Educational Leadership,* April 1993, pp. 13–15.

INDEX